PERSONAL DETAILS

Name

Address

Telephone

Email

Club/School Membership No.

Diving Qualifications

DIVED UP

Log Book No.

If you find this log book please contact the owner using the details above

ISBN 978-1-909455-06-1

Printed by Lightning Source.

Cover photo © Carson Grandi / Pocketstock.

Published 2013 by
Dived Up Publications
Oxford, United Kingdom
Email info@divedup.com
Web www.DivedUp.com

DIVED UP

FIT FOR UNDERWATER EXPLORING

DIVE LOG

DIVE No.

Date

Dive Site   Boat/Shore/Inland (circle)

Buddy   Purpose

Boat   Skipper   Port/Launch Site

| Dive No./Day | | Day in Sequence | | Surface Int. | : | Time in | : | out | : |

GAS	Mix	Pressure		Cyl. Size
		In	Out	
Bottom				
Travel				
Deco				

DIVE TIME	MAX DEPTH
mins	m/ft

Visibility

m/ft

Stops .... mins @ .... m/ft .... mins @ .... m/ft .... mins @ .... m/ft

Open Circuit [ ]   Semi-Closed [ ]   Closed Circuit [ ]   **Comp/Tables** ....

Weight .... kg/lbs **OK:** Y / N **(Add/Remove** .... **)**

Suit/Undersuit .... **Gloves** Y / N   **Hood** Y / N   **Hot / Cold / OK**

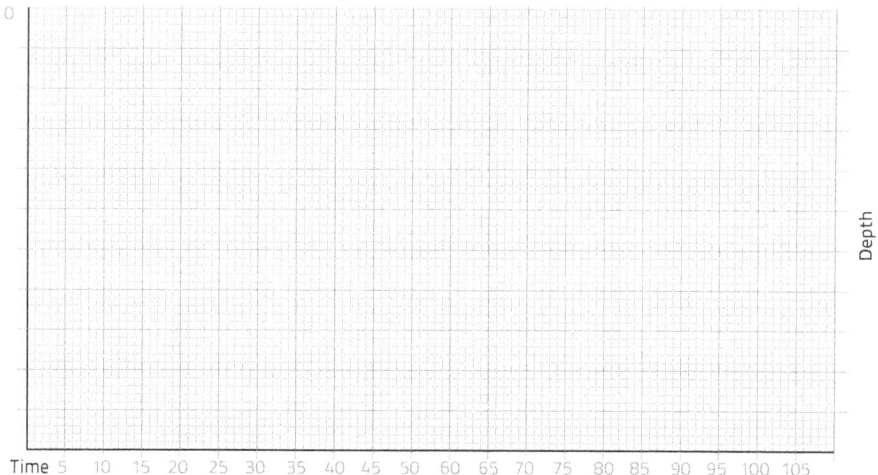

Time 5   10   15   20   25   30   35   40   45   50   55   60   65   70   75   80   85   90   95   100   105

Depth

Summary

Description/Sketch

Water Speed Slack / Slow / Steady / Fast   Temp @ Depth

Sea State   Wind Speed   Temp@ Surface

Kit/Skills Notes

Accumulated Dive Time   :   Milestone?

Verified by

     Signature   No.

| DIVE No. | DIVE LOG | Date |

Dive Site
Boat/Shore/Inland (circle)

| Buddy | Purpose |

| Boat | Skipper | Port/Launch Site |

| Dive No./Day | | Day in Sequence | | Surface Int. | : | Time in | : | out | : |

GAS	Mix	Pressure		Cyl. Size
		In	Out	
Bottom				
Travel				
Deco				

DIVE TIME

mins

MAX DEPTH

m/ft

Visibility

m/ft

Stops .... mins @ .... m/ft .... mins @ .... m/ft .... mins @ .... m/ft

Open Circuit ____ **Semi-Closed** ____ **Closed Circuit** ____ **Comp/Tables** ....

Weight .... kg/lbs **OK:** Y / N **(Add/Remove** .... **)**

Suit/Undersuit .... **Gloves** Y / N **Hood** Y / N **Hot / Cold / OK**

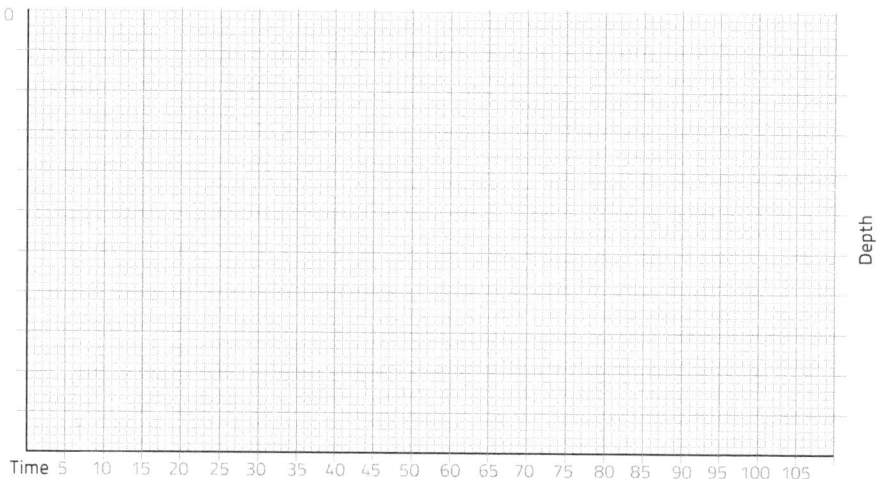

0

Depth

Time 5   10   15   20   25   30   35   40   45   50   60   65   70   75   80   85   90   95   100 105

Summary

Description/Sketch

DIVED UP

Water Speed Slack / Slow / Steady / Fast

Sea State   Wind Speed

Temp @ Depth

Temp@ Surface

Kit/Skills Notes

Accumulated Dive Time   :

Milestone?

Verified by

Signature   No.

DIVE No.	**DIVE LOG**	Date

Dive Site   Boat/Shore/Inland (circle)

Buddy   Purpose

Boat   Skipper   Port/Launch Site

Dive No./Day		Day in Sequence		Surface Int.	:	Time in	:	out	:

GAS	Mix	Pressure		Cyl. Size
		In	Out	
Bottom				
Travel				
Deco				

DIVE TIME	**MAX DEPTH**
mins	m/ft

Visibility
                                                                  m/ft

Stops .... mins @ .... m/ft .... mins @ .... m/ft .... mins @ .... m/ft

Open Circuit ☐   **Semi-Closed** ☐   **Closed Circuit** ☐   **Comp/Tables** ....
Weight .... kg/lbs   **OK:** Y / N   **(Add/Remove** .... **)**
Suit/Undersuit .... **Gloves** Y / N   **Hood** Y / N   **Hot / Cold / OK**

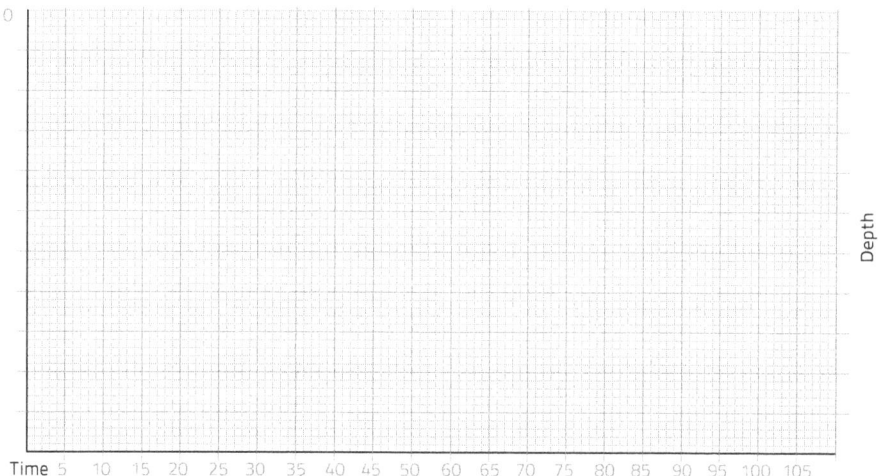

0

Depth

Time 5 10 15 20 25 30 35 40 45 50 55 60 65 70 75 80 85 90 95 100 105

Summary

Description/Sketch

DIVED UP

Water Speed   Slack / Slow / Steady / Fast   Temp @ Depth

Sea State   Wind Speed   Temp@ Surface

Kit/Skills Notes

Accumulated Dive Time   :   Milestone?

Verified by

                                    Signature   No.

DIVE No.	DIVE LOG	Date

Dive Site Boat/Shore/Inland (circle)

Buddy Purpose

Boat Skipper Port/Launch Site

Dive No./Day	Day in Sequence	Surface Int. :	Time in : out :

GAS	Mix	Pressure		Cyl. Size
		In	Out	
Bottom				
Travel				
Deco				

DIVE TIME .... mins   **MAX DEPTH** .... m/ft

Visibility .... m/ft

Stops .... mins @ .... m/ft   .... mins @ .... m/ft   .... mins @ .... m/ft

Open Circuit	Semi-Closed	Closed Circuit	Comp/Tables

Weight ....kg/lbs **OK:** Y / N **(Add/Remove** ....**)**

Suit/Undersuit ....**Gloves** Y / N   **Hood** Y / N   **Hot / Cold / OK**

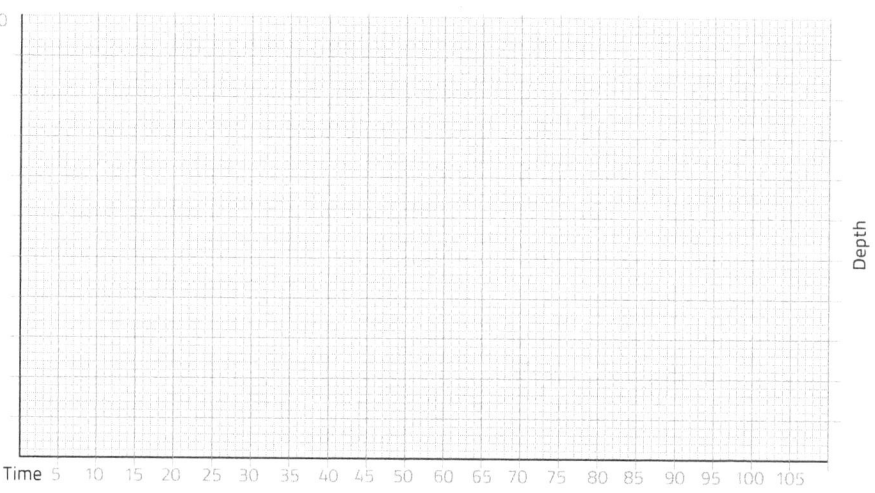

Time 5   10   15   20   25   30   35   40   45   50   55   60   65   70   75   80   85   90   95   100   105

Depth

Summary

Description/Sketch

DIVED UP

Water Speed   Slack / Slow / Steady / Fast   Temp @ Depth

Sea State   Wind Speed   Temp @ Surface

Kit/Skills Notes

Accumulated Dive Time   :   Milestone?

Verified by
                                    Signature   No.

| DIVE No. | **DIVE LOG** | Date |

Dive Site
Boat/Shore/Inland (circle)

Buddy Purpose

Boat Skipper Port/Launch Site

| Dive No./Day | Day in Sequence | Surface Int. | : | Time in | : | out | : |

GAS	Mix	Pressure		Cyl. Size	**DIVE TIME**	**MAX DEPTH**
		In	Out			
Bottom						
Travel					mins	m/ft
Deco					**Visibility**	
						m/ft

Stops .... mins @ .... m/ft .... mins @ .... m/ft .... mins @ .... m/ft

Open Circuit   **Semi-Closed**   **Closed Circuit**   **Comp/Tables** ....
Weight .... kg/lbs   **OK:** Y / N   **(Add/Remove** .... **)**
Suit/Undersuit .... **Gloves** Y / N   **Hood** Y / N   **Hot / Cold / OK**

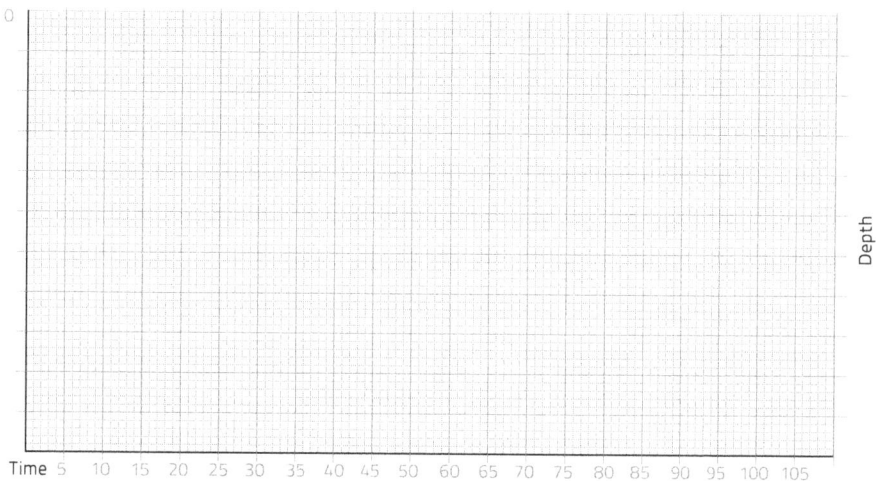

0

Depth

Time 5   10   15   20   25   30   35   40   45   50   60   65   70   75   80   85   90   95   100   105

Summary

Description/Sketch

DIVED UP

Water Speed   Slack / Slow / Steady / Fast   Temp @ Depth
Sea State   Wind Speed   Temp @ Surface

Kit/Skills Notes

Accumulated Dive Time   :   Milestone?

Verified by

                                        Signature   No.

| DIVE No. | DIVE LOG | Date |

Dive Site
Boat/Shore/Inland (circle)

| Buddy | Purpose |

| Boat | Skipper | Port/Launch Site |

| Dive No./Day | | Day in Sequence | | Surface Int. | : | Time in | : | out | : |

GAS	Mix	Pressure		Cyl. Size
		In	Out	
Bottom				
Travel				
Deco				

DIVE TIME

mins

MAX DEPTH

m/ft

Visibility
m/ft

Stops .... mins @ .... m/ft .... mins @ .... m/ft .... mins @ .... m/ft

Open Circuit   Semi-Closed   Closed Circuit   Comp/Tables ....
Weight .... kg/lbs **OK:** Y / N **(Add/Remove** .... **)**
Suit/Undersuit .... **Gloves** Y / N   **Hood** Y / N   **Hot / Cold / OK**

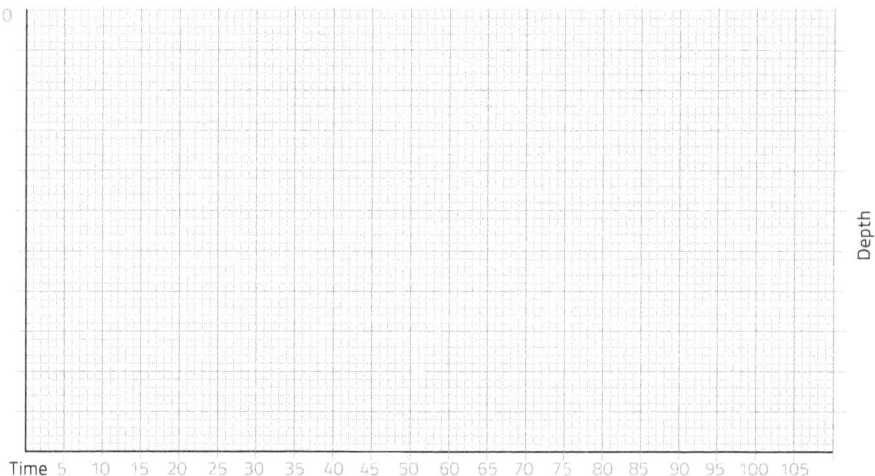

Time 5 10 15 20 25 30 35 40 45 50 60 65 70 75 80 85 90 95 100 105

Depth

Summary

Description/Sketch

DIVED UP

Water Speed Slack / Slow / Steady / Fast   Temp @ Depth

Sea State   Wind Speed   Temp@ Surface

Kit/Skills Notes

Accumulated Dive Time   :   Milestone?

Verified by

                                          Signature   No.

DIVE LOG

DIVE No.

Date

Dive Site

Boat/Shore/Inland (circle)

Buddy

Purpose

Boat

Skipper

Port/Launch Site

| Dive No./Day | | Day in Sequence | | Surface Int | : | Time in | : | out | : |

GAS	Mix	Pressure		Cyl. Size
		In	Out	
Bottom				
Travel				
Deco				

DIVE TIME

mins

MAX DEPTH

m/ft

Visibility

m/ft

Stops .... mins @ .... m/ft .... mins @ .... m/ft .... mins @ .... m/ft

| Open Circuit | Semi-Closed | Closed Circuit | Comp/Tables |

Weight ....kg/lbs **OK:** Y / N **(Add/Remove** ....**)**

Suit/Undersuit .... **Gloves** Y / N **Hood** Y / N **Hot / Cold / OK**

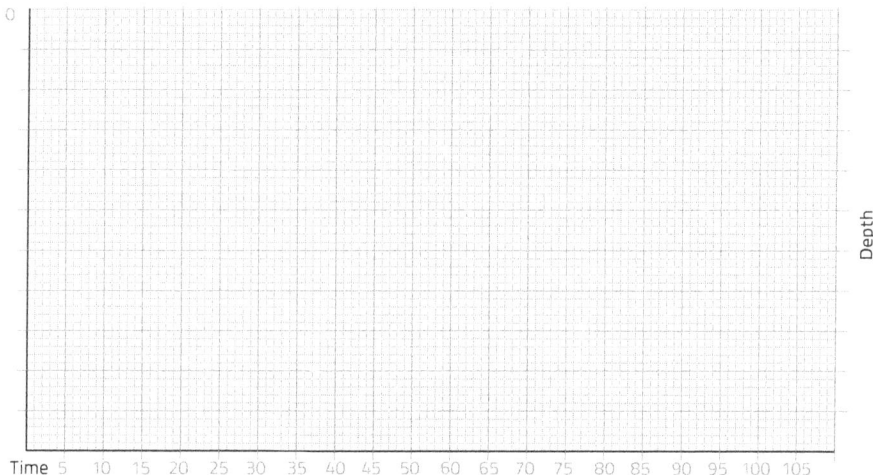

Depth

Time 5   10   15   20   25   30   35   40   45   50   55   60   65   70   75   80   85   90   95   100   105

Summary

Description/Sketch

DIVED UP

| Water Speed | Slack / Slow / Steady / Fast | Temp @ Depth |
| Sea State | Wind Speed | Temp@ Surface |

Kit/Skills Notes

| Accumulated Dive Time | : | Milestone? |

Verified by

Signature   No.

DIVE LOG

DIVE No.

Date

Dive Site   Boat/Shore/Inland (circle)

Buddy   **Purpose**

Boat   **Skipper**   **Port/Launch Site**

| Dive No./Day | | Day in Sequence | | Surface Int. | : | Time in | : | out | : |

GAS	Mix	Pressure		Cyl. Size
		In	Out	
Bottom				
Travel				
Deco				

DIVE TIME   **MAX DEPTH**

mins   m/ft

Visibility

m/ft

Stops .... mins @ .... m/ft .... mins @ .... m/ft .... mins @ .... m/ft

Open Circuit   **Semi-Closed**   **Closed Circuit**   **Comp/Tables** ....
Weight .... kg/lbs **OK:** Y / N **(Add/Remove** .... **)**
Suit/Undersuit .... **Gloves** Y / N **Hood** Y / N **Hot / Cold / OK**

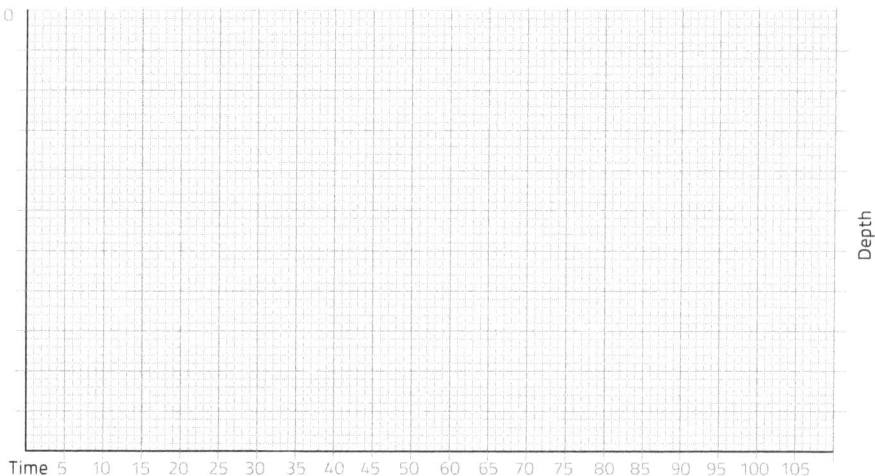

0

Depth

Time 5   10   15   20   25   30   35   40   45   50   55   60   65   70   75   80   85   90   95   100 105

Summary

Description/Sketch

Water Speed Slack / Slow / Steady / Fast   Temp @ Depth

Sea State   Wind Speed   Temp@ Surface

Kit/Skills Notes

Accumulated Dive Time   :   Milestone?

Verified by

Signature   No.

| DIVE No. | **DIVE LOG** | Date |

| **Dive Site** | Boat/Shore/Inland (circle) |

| Buddy | Purpose |

| Boat | Skipper | Port/Launch Site |

| Dive No./Day | Day in Sequence | Surface Int. : | Time in : | out : |

GAS	Mix	Pressure		Cyl. Size
		In	Out	
Bottom				
Travel				
Deco				

DIVE TIME

mins

MAX DEPTH

m/ft

Visibility

m/ft

Stops .... mins @ .... m/ft .... mins @ .... m/ft .... mins @ .... m/ft

| Open Circuit | Semi-Closed | Closed Circuit | Comp/Tables .... |

Weight .... kg/lbs **OK:** Y / N **(Add/Remove** .... **)**

Suit/Undersuit .... **Gloves** Y / N **Hood** Y / N **Hot / Cold / OK**

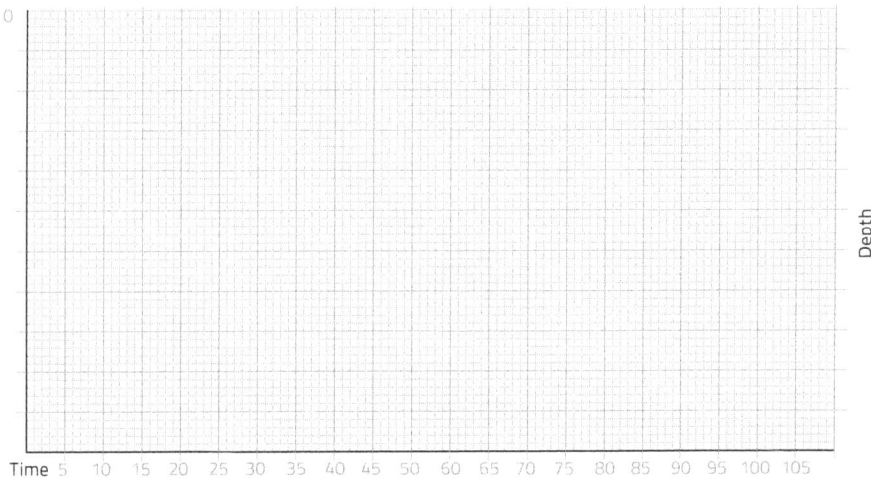

0

Depth

Time 5 10 15 20 25 30 35 40 45 50 55 60 65 70 75 80 85 90 95 100 105

Summary

Description/Sketch

DIVED UP

Water Speed   Slack / Slow / Steady / Fast   Temp @ Depth
Sea State   Wind Speed   Temp@ Surface

Kit/Skills Notes

Accumulated Dive Time	:	Milestone?

Verified by

Signature   No.

| DIVE No. | DIVE LOG | Date |

Dive Site
Boat/Shore/Inland (circle)

| Buddy | Purpose |

| Boat | Skipper | Port/Launch Site |

| Dive No./Day | | Day in Sequence | | Surface Int. | : | Time in | : | out | : |

GAS	Mix	Pressure		Cyl. Size
		In	Out	
Bottom				
Travel				
Deco				

DIVE TIME	MAX DEPTH
mins	m/ft

Visibility
m/ft

Stops .... mins @ .... m/ft .... mins @ .... m/ft .... mins @ .... m/ft

| Open Circuit | Semi-Closed | Closed Circuit | Comp/Tables |

Weight .... kg/lbs **OK:** Y / N (Add/Remove ....)

Suit/Undersuit .... **Gloves** Y / N **Hood** Y / N **Hot / Cold / OK**

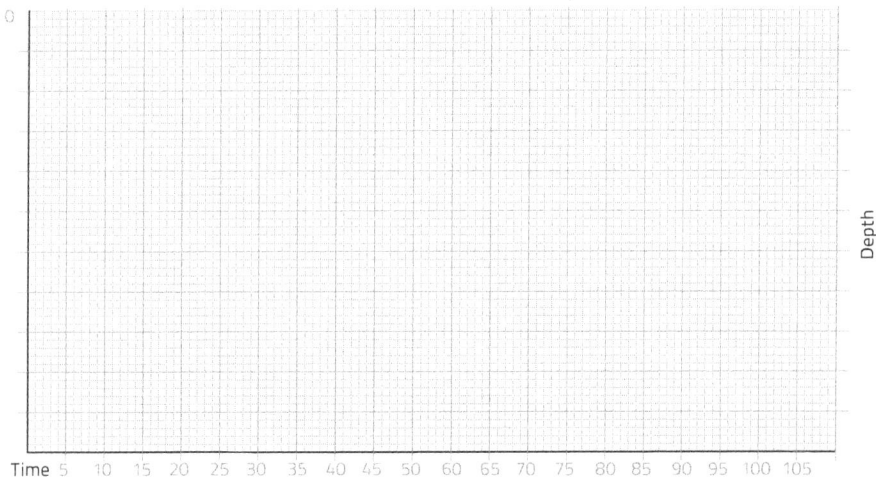

Depth

Time 5 10 15 20 25 30 35 40 45 50 55 60 65 70 75 80 85 90 95 100 105

Summary

Description/Sketch

DIVED UP

| Water Speed Slack / Slow / Steady / Fast | Temp @ Depth |
| Sea State | Wind Speed | Temp@ Surface |

Kit/Skills Notes

| Accumulated Dive Time | : | Milestone? |

Verified by

Signature   No.

DIVE No.	**DIVE LOG**	Date

Dive Site   Boat/Shore/Inland (circle)

Buddy   Purpose

Boat   Skipper   Port/Launch Site

Dive No./Day	Day in Sequence	Surface Int. :	Time in :	out :

GAS	Mix	Pressure		Cyl. Size	DIVE TIME	MAX DEPTH
		In	Out			
Bottom						
Travel					mins	m/ft
Deco					**Visibility**	
						m/ft

Stops .... mins @ .... m/ft .... mins @ .... m/ft .... mins @ .... m/ft

Open Circuit   **Semi-Closed**   **Closed Circuit**   **Comp/Tables** ....
Weight .... kg/lbs   **OK:** Y / N   **(Add/Remove** .... **)**
Suit/Undersuit .... **Gloves** Y / N   **Hood** Y / N   **Hot / Cold / OK**

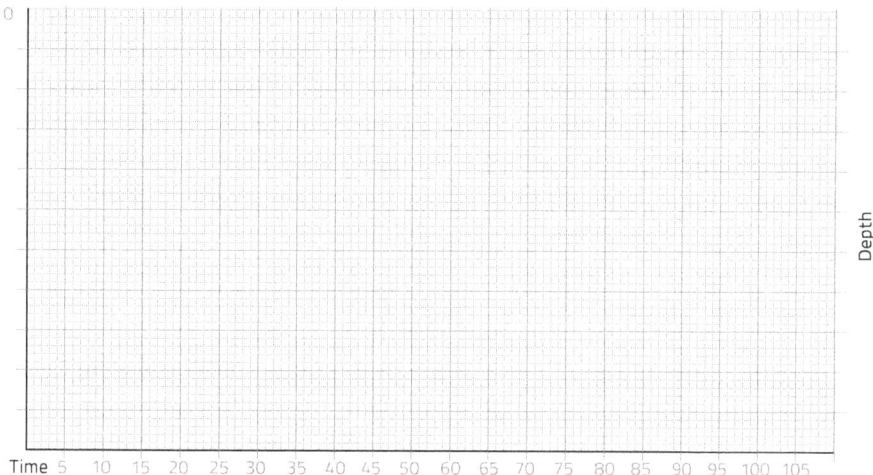

Depth

Time   5   10   15   20   25   30   35   40   45   50   55   60   65   70   75   80   85   90   95   100   105

Summary

Description/Sketch

DIVED UP

Water Speed   Slack / Slow / Steady / Fast   Temp @ Depth
Sea State   Wind Speed   Temp@ Surface

Kit/Skills Notes

Accumulated Dive Time   :   Milestone?

Verified by

Signature   No.

DIVE No.	**DIVE LOG**	Date

Dive Site   Boat/Shore/Inland (circle)

Buddy   Purpose

Boat   Skipper   Port/Launch Site

| Dive No./Day | | Day in Sequence | | Surface Int. | : | Time in | : | out | : |

GAS	Mix	Pressure		Cyl. Size
		In	Out	
Bottom				
Travel				
Deco				

DIVE TIME	MAX DEPTH
mins	m/ft

Visibility
m/ft

Stops .... mins @ .... m/ft .... mins @ .... m/ft .... mins @ .... m/ft

Open Circuit ☐   Semi-Closed ☐   Closed Circuit ☐   Comp/Tables ....

Weight ....kg/lbs   **OK:** Y / N   (Add/Remove ....)

Suit/Undersuit .... Gloves Y / N   Hood Y / N   Hot / Cold / OK

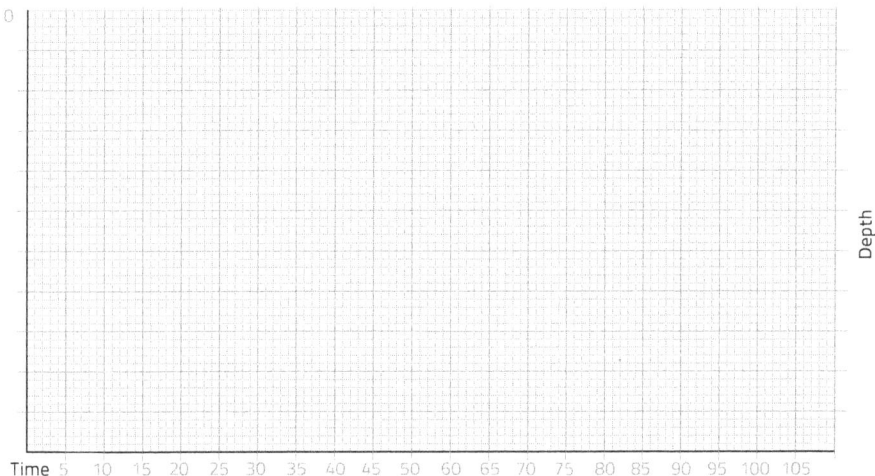

0

Depth

Time 5 10 15 20 25 30 35 40 45 50 60 65 70 75 80 85 90 95 100 105

Summary

Description/Sketch

DIVED UP

Water Speed Slack / Slow / Steady / Fast   Temp @ Depth

Sea State   Wind Speed   Temp@ Surface

Kit/Skills Notes

Accumulated Dive Time   :   Milestone?

Verified by

                              Signature   No.

DIVE LOG

DIVE No.

Date

Dive Site   Boat/Shore/Inland (circle)

Buddy   Purpose

Boat   Skipper   Port/Launch Site

Dive No./Day		Day in Sequence		Surface int.	:	Time in	:	out	:

GAS	Mix	Pressure		Cyl. Size
		In	Out	
Bottom				
Travel				
Deco				

DIVE TIME

mins

MAX DEPTH

m/ft

Visibility

m/ft

Stops .... mins @ .... m/ft .... mins @ .... m/ft .... mins @ .... m/ft

Open Circuit	Semi-Closed	Closed Circuit	Comp/Tables ....

Weight .... kg/lbs **OK:** Y / N **(Add/Remove** .... **)**

Suit/Undersuit .... **Gloves** Y / N **Hood** Y / N **Hot / Cold / OK**

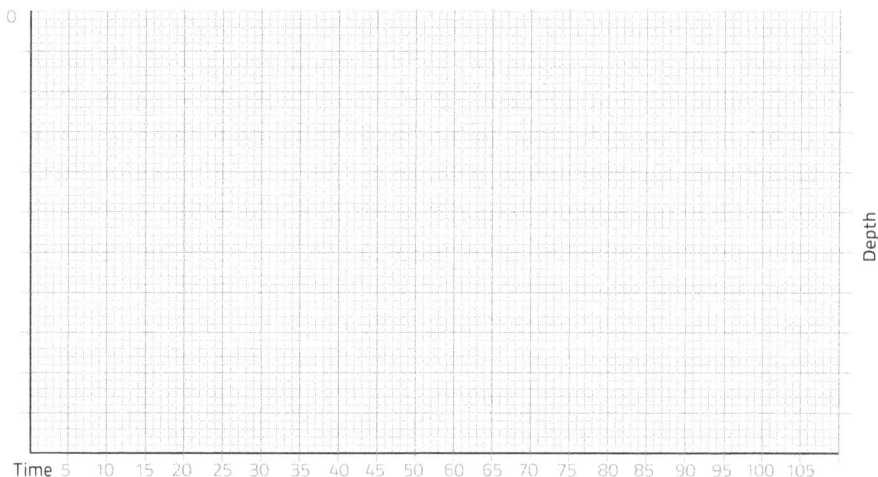

0

Depth

Time 5 10 15 20 25 30 35 40 45 50 55 60 65 70 75 80 85 90 95 100 105

Summary

Description/Sketch

DIVED UP

Water Speed   Slack / Slow / Steady / Fast   Temp @ Depth
Sea State   Wind Speed   Temp@ Surface

Kit/Skills Notes

Accumulated Dive Time   :   Milestone?

Verified by
                                 Signature   No.

| DIVE No. | **DIVE LOG** | Date |

Dive Site
Boat/Shore/Inland (circle)

Buddy
Purpose

Boat
Skipper
Port/Launch Site

| Dive No./Day | | Day in Sequence | | Surface Int. | : | Time in | : | out | : |

GAS	Mix	Pressure		Cyl. Size	DIVE TIME	MAX DEPTH
		In	Out			
Bottom						
Travel						
Deco					mins	m/ft

Visibility
m/ft

Stops .... mins @ .... m/ft .... mins @ .... m/ft .... mins @ .... m/ft

| Open Circuit | Semi-Closed | Closed Circuit | Comp/Tables .... |

Weight .... kg/lbs **OK:** Y / N **(Add/Remove** .... **)**

Suit/Undersuit .... **Gloves** Y / N **Hood** Y / N **Hot / Cold / OK**

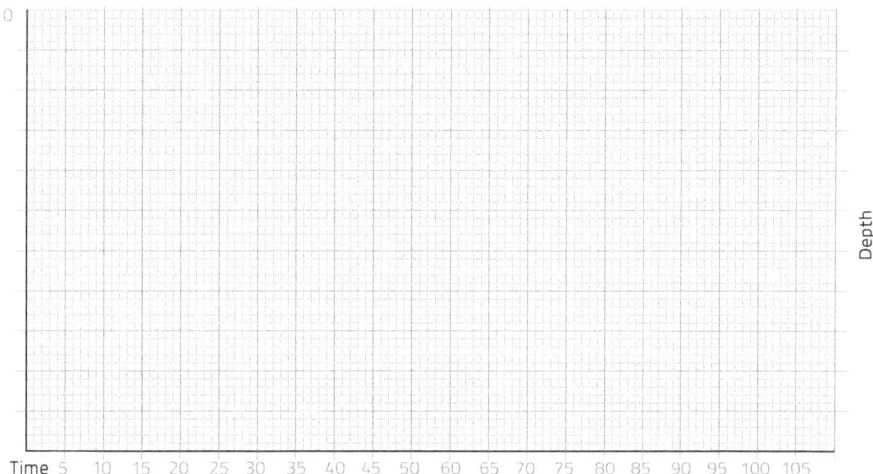

Depth

Time 5 10 15 20 25 30 35 40 45 50 55 60 65 70 75 80 85 90 95 100 105

Summary

Description/Sketch

DIVED UP

Water Speed Slack / Slow / Steady / Fast   Temp @ Depth

Sea State   Wind Speed   Temp@ Surface

Kit/Skills Notes

Accumulated Dive Time   :   Milestone?

Verified by

Signature   No.

DIVE No.	DIVE LOG	Date

Dive Site   Boat/Shore/Inland (circle)

Buddy   Purpose

Boat   Skipper   Port/Launch Site

Dive No./Day		Day in Sequence		Surface Int.	:	Time in	:	out	:

GAS	Mix	Pressure		Cyl. Size
		In	Out	
Bottom				
Travel				
Deco				

DIVE TIME	MAX DEPTH
mins	m/ft

Visibility   m/ft

Stops .... mins @ .... m/ft .... mins @ .... m/ft .... mins @ .... m/ft

Open Circuit   Semi-Closed   Closed Circuit   Comp/Tables ....

Weight .... kg/lbs   **OK:** Y / N   **(Add/Remove** .... **)**

Suit/Undersuit .... Gloves Y / N   Hood Y / N   Hot / Cold / OK

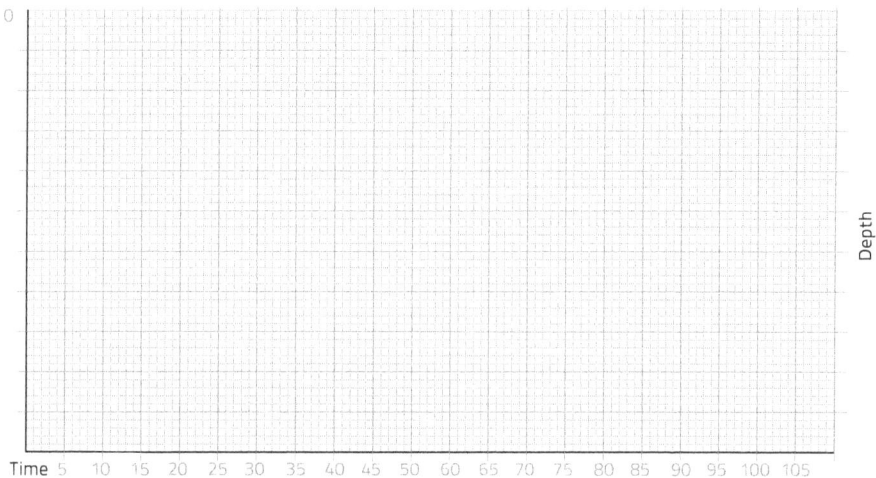

0

Depth

Time 5   10   15   20   25   30   35   40   45   50   60   65   70   75   80   85   90   95   100   105

Summary

Description/Sketch

Water Speed Slack / Slow / Steady / Fast   Temp @ Depth

Sea State   Wind Speed   Temp@ Surface

Kit/Skills Notes

Accumulated Dive Time   :   Milestone?

Verified by

                                    Signature   No.

DIVE No.   **DIVE LOG**   **Date**

Dive Site   Boat/Shore/Inland (circle)

Buddy   Purpose

Boat   Skipper   Port/Launch Site

Dive No./Day | Day in Sequence | Surface Int. | : | Time in | : | out | :

GAS	Mix	Pressure		Cyl. Size	**DIVE TIME**	**MAX DEPTH**
		In	Out			
Bottom						
Travel					mins	m/ft
Deco					**Visibility**	m/ft

Stops .... mins @ .... m/ft .... mins @ .... m/ft .... mins @ .... m/ft

Open Circuit | Semi-Closed | Closed Circuit | Comp/Tables ....
Weight ....kg/lbs **OK:** Y / N **(Add/Remove** ....**)**
Suit/Undersuit .... **Gloves** Y / N **Hood** Y / N **Hot / Cold / OK**

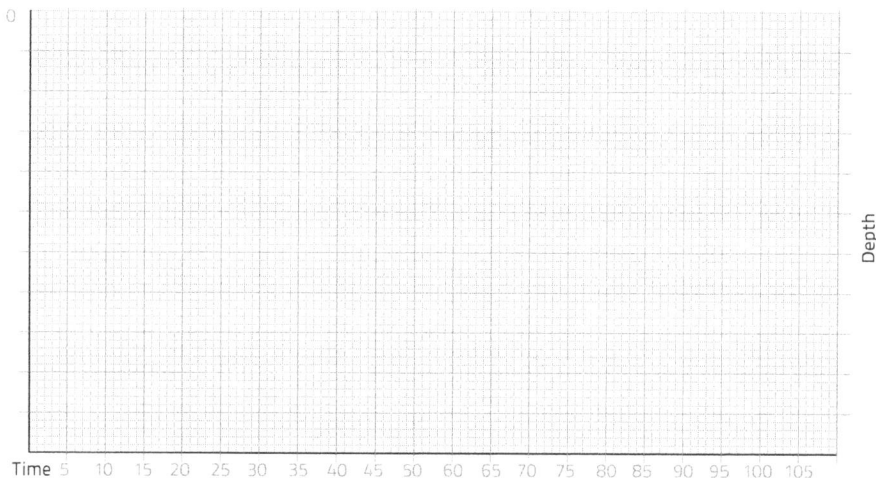

Depth

Time 5   10   15   20   25   30   35   40   45   50   60   65   70   75   80   85   90   95   100 105

Summary

Description/Sketch

(blank lined space)

DIVED UP

Water Speed Slack / Slow / Steady / Fast		Temp @ Depth
Sea State	Wind Speed	Temp@ Surface

Kit/Skills Notes

Accumulated Dive Time :	Milestone?

Verified by

Signature   No.

DIVE LOG

DIVE No.

Date

Dive Site　　　　　　　　　　　　　　　　　Boat/Shore/Inland (circle)

Buddy　　　　　　　　　　　　　　**Purpose**

Boat　　　　　　　**Skipper**　　　　　**Port/Launch Site**

Dive No./Day		Day in Sequence		Surface Int.	:	Time in	:	out	:

GAS	Mix	Pressure		Cyl. Size
		In	Out	
Bottom				
Travel				
Deco				

DIVE TIME

mins

MAX DEPTH

m/ft

Visibility

m/ft

Stops .... mins @ .... m/ft .... mins @ .... m/ft .... mins @ .... m/ft

Open Circuit　　**Semi-Closed**　　**Closed Circuit**　　　**Comp/Tables** ....
Weight ....kg/lbs　**OK:** Y / N　**(Add/Remove** ....**)**
Suit/Undersuit .... **Gloves** Y / N　**Hood** Y / N　**Hot / Cold / OK**

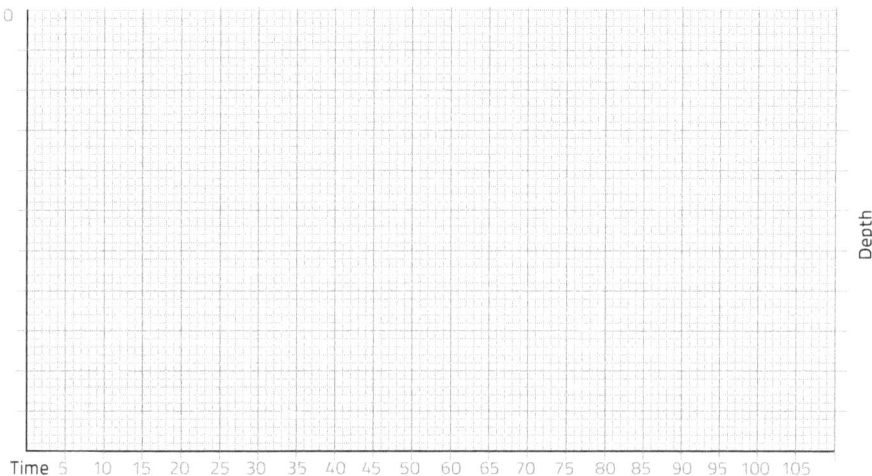

0

Depth

Time 5　10　15　20　25　30　35　40　45　50　60　65　70　75　80　85　90　95　100　105

Summary

Description/Sketch

DIVED UP

Water Speed Slack / Slow / Steady / Fast   Temp @ Depth

Sea State   Wind Speed   Temp@ Surface

Kit/Skills Notes

Accumulated Dive Time   :   Milestone?

Verified by

Signature   No.

DIVE No.	DIVE LOG	Date

Dive Site — Boat/Shore/Inland (circle)

Buddy — Purpose

Boat — Skipper — Port/Launch Site

Dive No./Day		Day in Sequence		Surface Int.	:	Time in	:	out	:

GAS	Mix	Pressure		Cyl. Size	DIVE TIME	MAX DEPTH
		In	Out			
Bottom						
Travel						
Deco					mins	m/ft

DIVE TIME ___ mins **MAX DEPTH** ___ m/ft

Visibility ___ m/ft

Stops .... mins @ .... m/ft .... mins @ .... m/ft .... mins @ .... m/ft

Open Circuit ☐ Semi-Closed ☐ Closed Circuit ☐ Comp/Tables _____

Weight .... kg/lbs **OK:** Y / N (Add/Remove ....)

Suit/Undersuit .... Gloves Y / N Hood Y / N Hot / Cold / OK

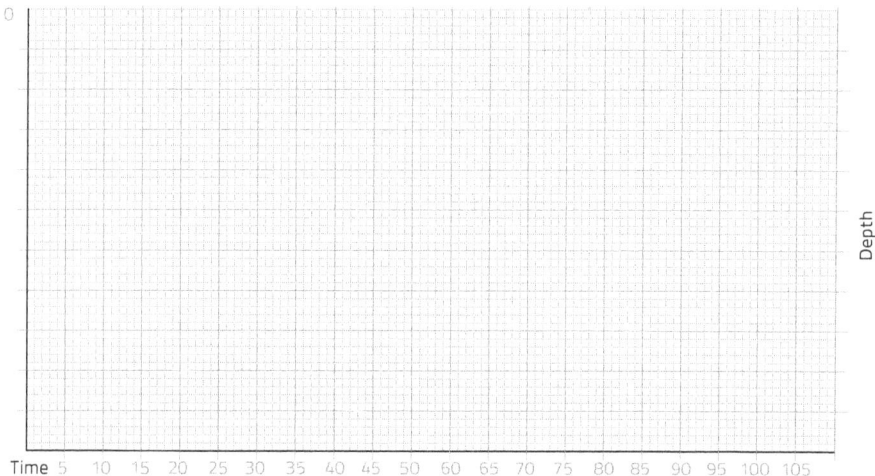

Time 5 10 15 20 25 30 35 40 45 50 60 65 70 75 80 85 90 95 100 105

Depth

Summary

Description/Sketch

DIVED UP

Water Speed Slack / Slow / Steady / Fast   Temp @ Depth

Sea State   Wind Speed   Temp@ Surface

Kit/Skills Notes

Accumulated Dive Time	:	Milestone?

Verified by

Signature   No.

DIVE LOG

DIVE No.

Date

Dive Site   Boat/Shore/Inland (circle)

Buddy   Purpose

Boat   Skipper   Port/Launch Site

| Dive No./Day | | Day in Sequence | | Surface Int. | : | Time in | : | out | : |

GAS	Mix	Pressure		Cyl. Size
		In	Out	
Bottom				
Travel				
Deco				

DIVE TIME
mins

MAX DEPTH
m/ft

Visibility
m/ft

Stops .... mins @ .... m/ft .... mins @ .... m/ft .... mins @ .... m/ft

Open Circuit ☐   Semi-Closed ☐   Closed Circuit ☐   Comp/Tables ....

Weight ....kg/lbs OK: Y / N (Add/Remove..................)

Suit/Undersuit ....Gloves Y / N Hood Y / N Hot / Cold / OK

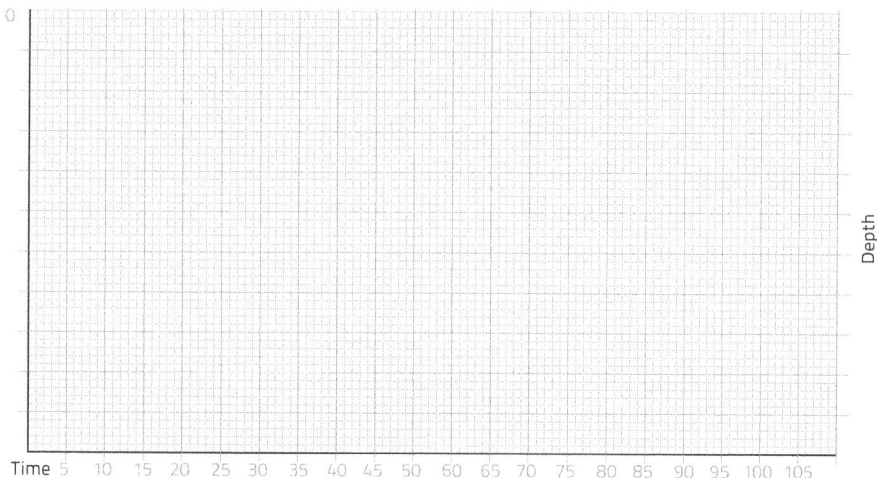

Depth

Time 5 10 15 20 25 30 35 40 45 50 55 60 65 70 75 80 85 90 95 100 105

Summary

Description/Sketch

DIVED UP

Water Speed Slack / Slow / Steady / Fast   Temp @ Depth

Sea State   Wind Speed   Temp@ Surface

Kit/Skills Notes

Accumulated Dive Time   :   Milestone?

Verified by

                                     Signature   No.

DIVE No.	DIVE LOG	Date

Dive Site   Boat/Shore/Inland (circle)

Buddy   Purpose

Boat   Skipper   Port/Launch Site

Dive No./Day		Day in Sequence		Surface Int.	:	Time in	:	out	:

GAS	Mix	Pressure		Cyl. Size	DIVE TIME	MAX DEPTH
		In	Out			
Bottom						
Travel						
Deco					mins	m/ft

Visibility

m/ft

Stops .... mins @ .... m/ft .... mins @ .... m/ft .... mins @ .... m/ft

Open Circuit [ ]   **Semi-Closed** [ ]   **Closed Circuit** [ ]   **Comp/Tables** ....
Weight .... kg/lbs   **OK:** Y / N   **(Add/Remove** .... **)**
Suit/Undersuit .... **Gloves** Y / N   **Hood** Y / N   **Hot / Cold / OK**

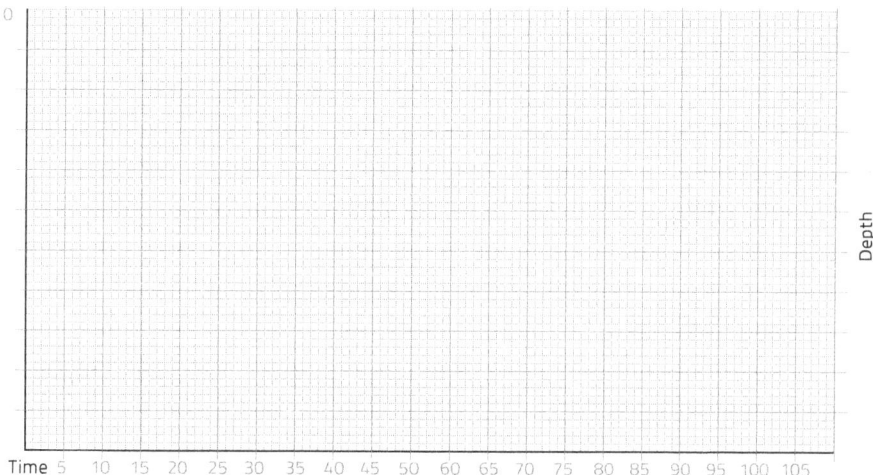

0

Depth

Time 5   10   15   20   25   30   35   40   45   50   60   65   70   75   80   85   90   95   100 105

Summary

Description/Sketch

DIVED UP

Water Speed Slack / Slow / Steady / Fast   Temp @ Depth

Sea State   Wind Speed   Temp@ Surface

Kit/Skills Notes

Accumulated Dive Time   :   Milestone?

Verified by

Signature   No.

DIVE No.	**DIVE LOG**	Date

Dive Site   Boat/Shore/Inland (circle)

Buddy   Purpose

Boat   Skipper   Port/Launch Site

Dive No./Day		Day in Sequence		Surface Int:	:	Time in	:	out	:

GAS	Mix	Pressure		Cyl. Size
		In	Out	
Bottom				
Travel				
Deco				

DIVE TIME   mins

MAX DEPTH   m/ft

Visibility   m/ft

Stops .... mins @ .... m/ft   .... mins @ .... m/ft   .... mins @ .... m/ft

Open Circuit   **Semi-Closed**   **Closed Circuit**   **Comp/Tables** ....

Weight ....kg/lbs   **OK:** Y / N   **(Add/Remove** .... **)**

Suit/Undersuit ....**Gloves** Y / N   **Hood** Y / N   **Hot / Cold / OK**

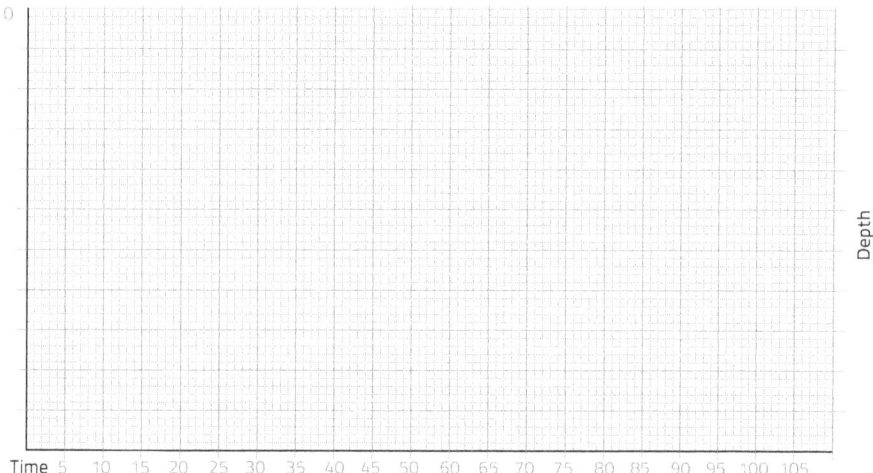

Depth

Time 5   10   15   20   25   30   35   40   45   50   55   60   65   70   75   80   85   90   95   100   105

Summary

Description/Sketch

DIVED UP

Water Speed	Slack / Slow / Steady / Fast		Temp @ Depth	
Sea State		Wind Speed	Temp@ Surface	

Kit/Skills Notes

Accumulated Dive Time	:	Milestone?

Verified by		
	Signature	No.

DIVE No.	**DIVE LOG**	Date

Dive Site — Boat/Shore/Inland (circle)

Buddy — Purpose

Boat — Skipper — Port/Launch Site

Dive No./Day		Day in Sequence		Surface Int.	:	Time in	:	out	:

GAS	Mix	Pressure		Cyl. Size	**DIVE TIME**	**MAX DEPTH**
		In	Out			
Bottom						
Travel						
Deco					mins	m/ft

Visibility m/ft

Stops .... mins @ .... m/ft .... mins @ .... m/ft .... mins @ .... m/ft

Open Circuit	Semi-Closed	Closed Circuit	Comp/Tables ....

Weight .... kg/lbs **OK:** Y / N **(Add/Remove** ....**)**

Suit/Undersuit .... **Gloves** Y / N **Hood** Y / N **Hot / Cold / OK**

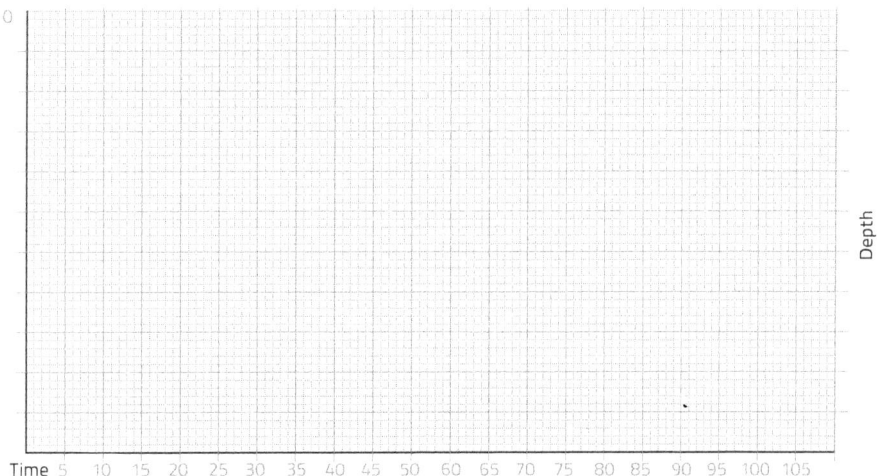

Time 5 10 15 20 25 30 35 40 45 50 55 60 65 70 75 80 85 90 95 100 105

Depth

Summary

Description/Sketch

DIVED UP

Water Speed Slack / Slow / Steady / Fast   Temp @ Depth

Sea State   Wind Speed   Temp@ Surface

Kit/Skills Notes

Accumulated Dive Time   :   Milestone?

Verified by

Signature   No.

DIVE LOG

DIVE No.

Date

Dive Site   Boat/Shore/Inland (circle)

Buddy   Purpose

Boat   Skipper   Port/Launch Site

| Dive No./Day | Day in Sequence | Surface Int. : | Time in : | out : |

GAS	Mix	Pressure		Cyl. Size
		In	Out	
Bottom				
Travel				
Deco				

DIVE TIME

MAX DEPTH

mins

m/ft

Visibility

m/ft

Stops .... mins @ .... m/ft .... mins @ .... m/ft .... mins @ .... m/ft

Open Circuit   **Semi-Closed**   **Closed Circuit**   **Comp/Tables** ....
Weight .... kg/lbs **OK:** Y / N **(Add/Remove** .... **)**
Suit/Undersuit .... **Gloves** Y / N **Hood** Y / N **Hot / Cold / OK**

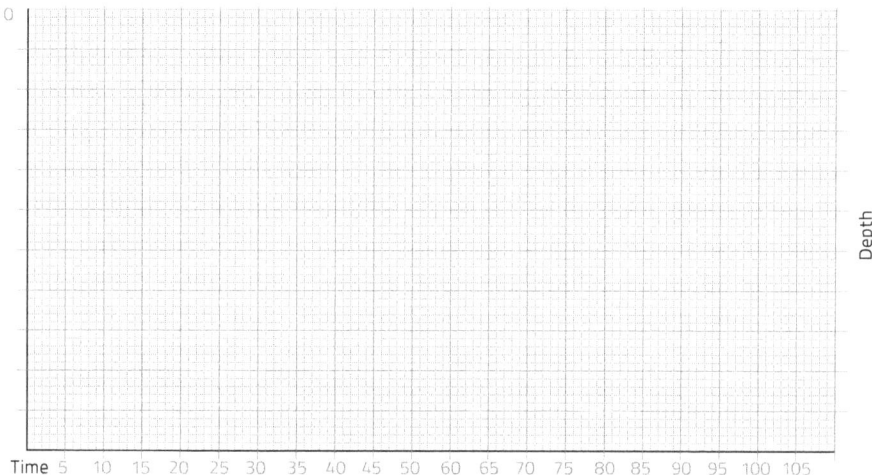

0

Depth

Time 5   10   15   20   25   30   35   40   45   50   60   65   70   75   80   85   90   95   100 105

Summary

Description/Sketch

DIVED UP

Water Speed Slack / Slow / Steady / Fast   Temp @ Depth

Sea State   Wind Speed   Temp@ Surface

Kit/Skills Notes

Accumulated Dive Time   :   Milestone?

Verified by

Signature   No.

DIVE No.		**DIVE LOG**		Date

Dive Site · Boat/Shore/Inland (circle)

Buddy · Purpose

Boat · Skipper · Port/Launch Site

Dive No./Day		Day in Sequence		Surface Int.	:	Time in	:	out	:

GAS	Mix	Pressure		Cyl. Size	DIVE TIME	MAX DEPTH
		In	Out			
Bottom						
Travel						
Deco					mins	m/ft

Visibility
m/ft

Stops .... mins @ .... m/ft .... mins @ .... m/ft .... mins @ .... m/ft

Open Circuit ☐ Semi-Closed ☐ Closed Circuit ☐ Comp/Tables ....

Weight .... kg/lbs OK: Y / N (Add/Remove ....)

Suit/Undersuit .... Gloves Y / N Hood Y / N Hot / Cold / OK

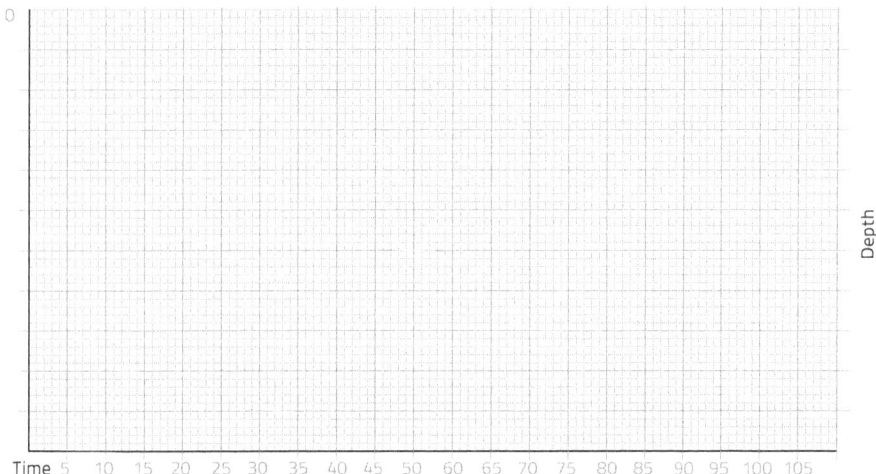

0

Depth

Time 5 10 15 20 25 30 35 40 45 50 55 60 65 70 75 80 85 90 95 100 105

Summary

Description/Sketch

DIVED UP

Water Speed   Slack / Slow / Steady / Fast   Temp @ Depth

Sea State   Wind Speed   Temp@ Surface

Kit/Skills Notes

Accumulated Dive Time   :   Milestone?

Verified by

Signature   No.

DIVE LOG

DIVE No.

Date

Dive Site

Boat/Shore/Inland (circle)

Buddy

Purpose

Boat

Skipper

Port/Launch Site

| Dive No./Day | | Day in Sequence | | Surface Int. | : | Time in | : | out | : |

GAS	Mix	Pressure		Cyl. Size
		In	Out	
Bottom				
Travel				
Deco				

DIVE TIME

mins

MAX DEPTH

m/ft

Visibility

m/ft

Stops .... mins @ .... m/ft .... mins @ .... m/ft .... mins @ .... m/ft

Open Circuit ☐ Semi-Closed ☐ Closed Circuit ☐ Comp/Tables ....

Weight ....kg/lbs **OK:** Y / N **(Add/Remove** ....**)**

Suit/Undersuit .... **Gloves** Y / N **Hood** Y / N **Hot / Cold / OK**

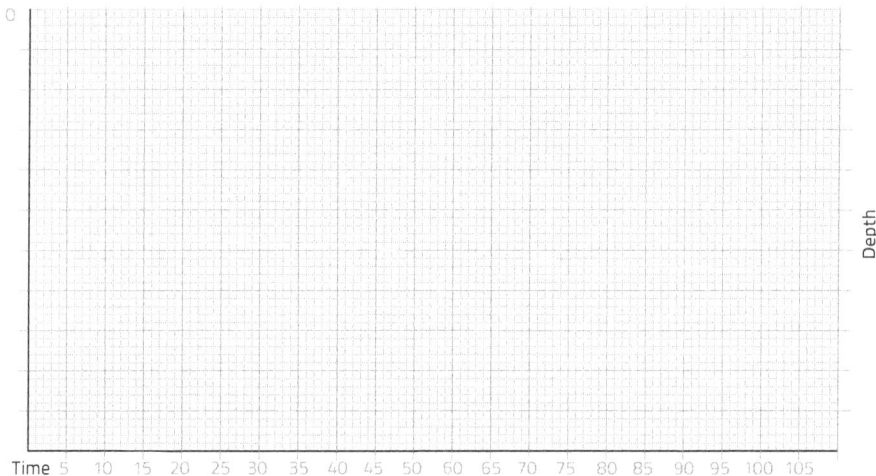

0

Depth

Time 5 10 15 20 25 30 35 40 45 50 60 65 70 75 80 85 90 95 100 105

Summary

Description/Sketch

DIVED UP

Water Speed Slack / Slow / Steady / Fast   Temp @ Depth

Sea State   Wind Speed   Temp @ Surface

Kit/Skills Notes

Accumulated Dive Time   :   Milestone?

Verified by

Signature   No.

DIVE No.	DIVE LOG	Date

Dive Site
Boat/Shore/Inland (circle)

Buddy
Purpose

Boat
Skipper — Port/Launch Site

Dive No./Day	Day in Sequence	Surface Int. :	Time in :	out :

GAS	Mix	Pressure		Cyl. Size	DIVE TIME	MAX DEPTH
		In	Out			
Bottom						
Travel					mins	m/ft
Deco						

Visibility
m/ft

Stops .... mins @ .... m/ft .... mins @ .... m/ft .... mins @ .... m/ft

Open Circuit ☐ Semi-Closed ☐ Closed Circuit ☐ Comp/Tables ....

Weight .... kg/lbs **OK:** Y / N **(Add/Remove** .... **)**

Suit/Undersuit .... **Gloves** Y / N **Hood** Y / N **Hot / Cold / OK**

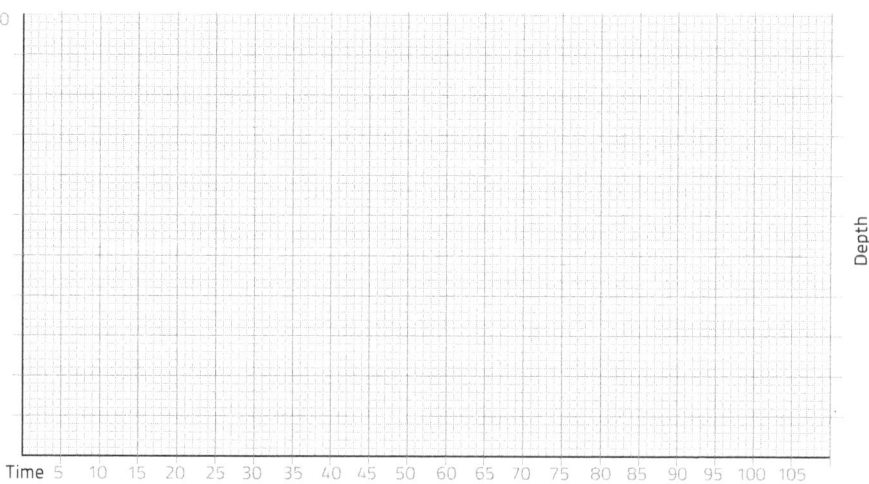

0

Depth

Time 5 10 15 20 25 30 35 40 45 50 60 65 70 75 80 85 90 95 100 105

Summary

Description/Sketch

Water Speed	Slack / Slow / Steady / Fast	Temp @ Depth
Sea State	Wind Speed	Temp@ Surface

Kit/Skills Notes

Accumulated Dive Time	:	Milestone?

Verified by

Signature   No.

DIVE LOG

DIVE No.

Date

Dive Site   Boat/Shore/Inland (circle)

Buddy   **Purpose**

Boat   **Skipper**   **Port/Launch Site**

| Dive No./Day | | Day in Sequence | | Surface Int. | : | Time in | : | out | : |

GAS	Mix	Pressure		Cyl. Size
		In	Out	
Bottom				
Travel				
Deco				

DIVE TIME   **MAX DEPTH**

mins   m/ft

Visibility

m/ft

Stops .... mins @ .... m/ft .... mins @ .... m/ft .... mins @ .... m/ft

Open Circuit ☐   Semi-Closed ☐   Closed Circuit ☐   Comp/Tables ....

Weight ....kg/lbs   **OK:** Y / N   **(Add/Remove** ....**)**

Suit/Undersuit ....**Gloves** Y / N   **Hood** Y / N   **Hot / Cold / OK**

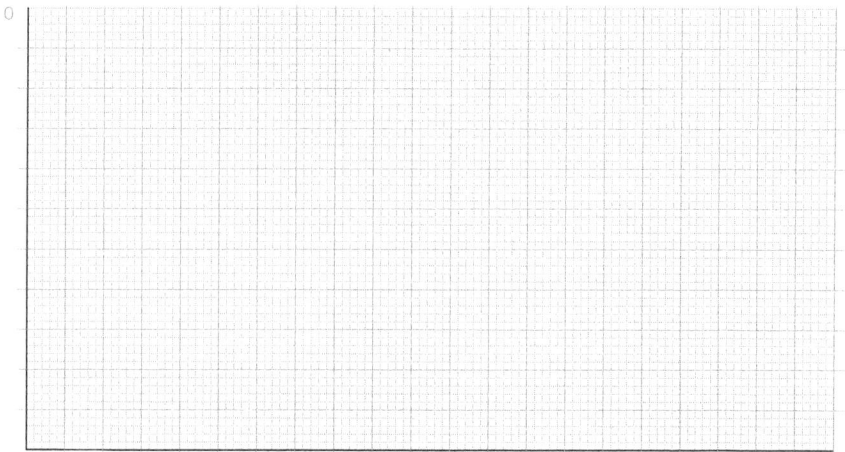

0

Depth

Time 5   10   15   20   25   30   35   40   45   50   60   65   70   75   80   85   90   95   100   105

Summary

Description/Sketch

_____
_____
_____
_____
_____
_____
_____
_____
_____
_____
_____
_____
_____

DIVED UP

Water Speed Slack / Slow / Steady / Fast		Temp @ Depth
Sea State	Wind Speed	Temp@ Surface

Kit/Skills Notes

Accumulated Dive Time :	Milestone?

Verified by

Signature   No.

DIVE No.	DIVE LOG	Date

Dive Site   Boat/Shore/Inland (circle)

Buddy   Purpose

Boat   Skipper   Port/Launch Site

Dive No./Day		Day in Sequence		Surface Int.	:	Time in	:	out	:

GAS	Mix	Pressure		Cyl. Size	DIVE TIME	MAX DEPTH
		In	Out			
Bottom						
Travel					mins	m/ft
Deco					**Visibility**	m/ft

Stops .... mins @ .... m/ft .... mins @ .... m/ft .... mins @ .... m/ft

Open Circuit ☐   Semi-Closed ☐   Closed Circuit ☐   Comp/Tables ....

Weight ....kg/lbs **OK:** Y / N   (Add/Remove ....)

Suit/Undersuit .... **Gloves** Y / N   **Hood** Y / N   **Hot / Cold / OK**

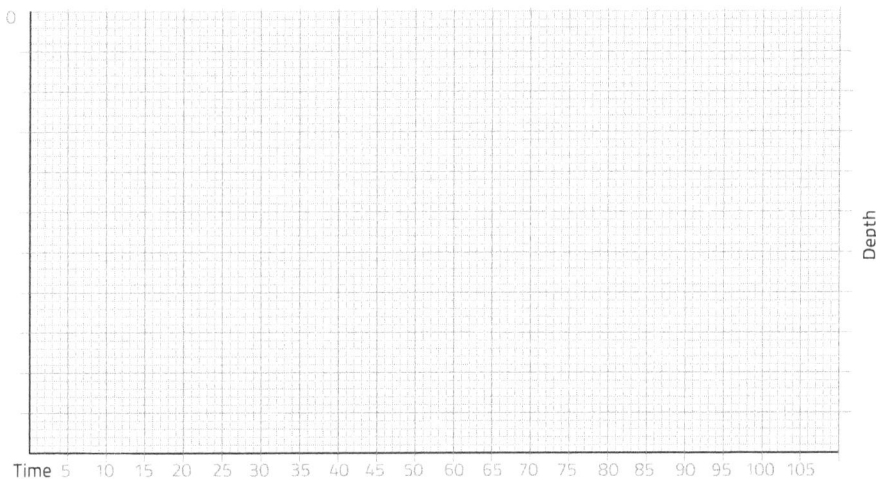

0

Depth

Time 5   10   15   20   25   30   35   40   45   50   55   60   65   70   75   80   85   90   95   100 105

Summary

Description/Sketch

DIVED UP

Water Speed Slack / Slow / Steady / Fast   Temp @ Depth

Sea State   Wind Speed   Temp@ Surface

Kit/Skills Notes

Accumulated Dive Time   :   Milestone?

Verified by

Signature   No.

| DIVE No. | **DIVE LOG** | Date |

Dive Site
Boat/Shore/Inland (circle)

Buddy
Purpose

Boat
Skipper — Port/Launch Site

| Dive No./Day | Day in Sequence | Surface Int. : | Time in : | out : |

GAS	Mix	Pressure		Cyl. Size	DIVE TIME	MAX DEPTH
		In	Out			
Bottom						
Travel						mins / m/ft
Deco						

Visibility m/ft

Stops .... mins @ .... m/ft .... mins @ .... m/ft .... mins @ .... m/ft

Open Circuit ☐   Semi-Closed ☐   Closed Circuit ☐   Comp/Tables ....

Weight .... kg/lbs   **OK:** Y / N   (Add/Remove ....)

Suit/Undersuit .... **Gloves** Y / N   **Hood** Y / N   **Hot / Cold / OK**

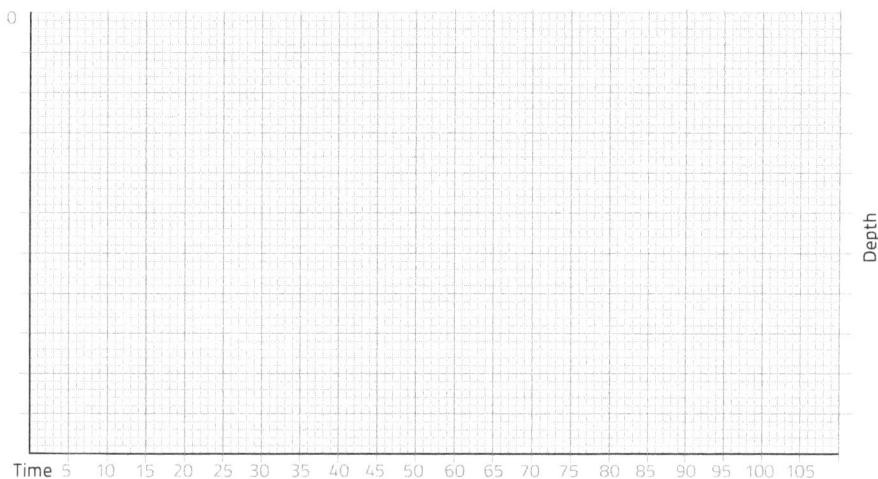

0

Depth

Time 5 10 15 20 25 30 35 40 45 50 55 60 65 70 75 80 85 90 95 100 105

Summary

Description/Sketch

DIVED UP

Water Speed	Slack / Slow / Steady / Fast		Temp @ Depth
Sea State		Wind Speed	Temp@ Surface

Kit/Skills Notes

Accumulated Dive Time	:	Milestone?

Verified by

Signature   No.

DIVE LOG

DIVE No.

Date

Dive Site   Boat/Shore/Inland (circle)

Buddy   Purpose

Boat   Skipper   Port/Launch Site

| Dive No./Day | | Day in Sequence | | Surface Int. | : | Time in | : | out | : |

GAS	Mix	Pressure		Cyl. Size
		In	Out	
Bottom				
Travel				
Deco				

DIVE TIME	**MAX DEPTH**
mins	m/ft

Visibility
                                                    m/ft

Stops .... mins @ .... m/ft   .... mins @ .... m/ft   .... mins @ .... m/ft

Open Circuit   **Semi-Closed**   **Closed Circuit**   **Comp/Tables** ....
Weight ....kg/lbs   **OK:** Y / N   **(Add/Remove** ....)
Suit/Undersuit ....**Gloves** Y / N   **Hood** Y / N   **Hot / Cold / OK**

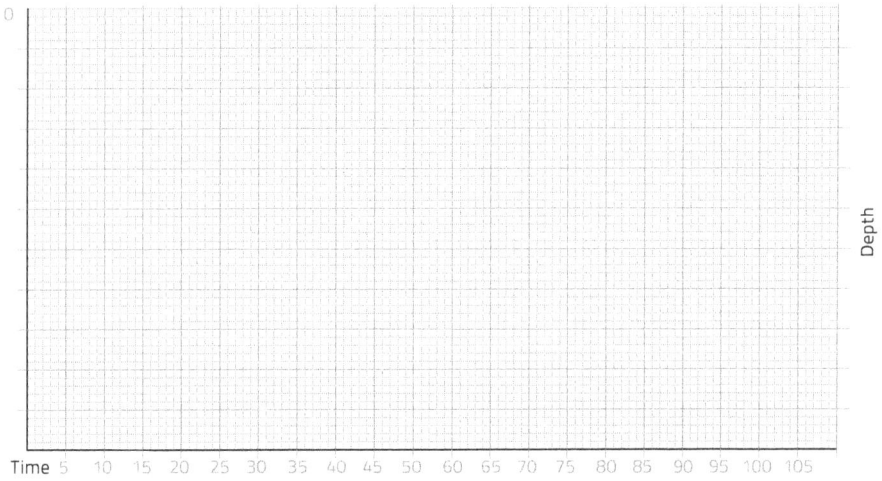

0

Depth

Time 5   10   15   20   25   30   35   40   45   50   60   65   70   75   80   85   90   95   100   105

Summary

Description/Sketch

DIVED UP

Water Speed	Slack / Slow / Steady / Fast		Temp @ Depth	
Sea State		Wind Speed	Temp@ Surface	

Kit/Skills Notes

Accumulated Dive Time	:	Milestone?

Verified by

Signature   No.

DIVE No.

Date

Dive Site

Boat/Shore/Inland (circle)

Buddy

Purpose

Boat

Skipper

Port/Launch Site

| Dive No./Day | | Day in Sequence | | Surface Int. | : | Time in | : | out | : |

GAS	Mix	Pressure		Cyl. Size
		In	Out	
Bottom				
Travel				
Deco				

DIVE TIME

mins

MAX DEPTH

m/ft

Visibility

m/ft

Stops .... mins @ .... m/ft .... mins @ .... m/ft .... mins @ .... m/ft

Open Circuit   **Semi-Closed**   **Closed Circuit**   **Comp/Tables** ....

Weight ....kg/lbs   **OK:** Y / N   **(Add/Remove** .... **)**

Suit/Undersuit ....**Gloves** Y / N   **Hood** Y / N   **Hot / Cold / OK**

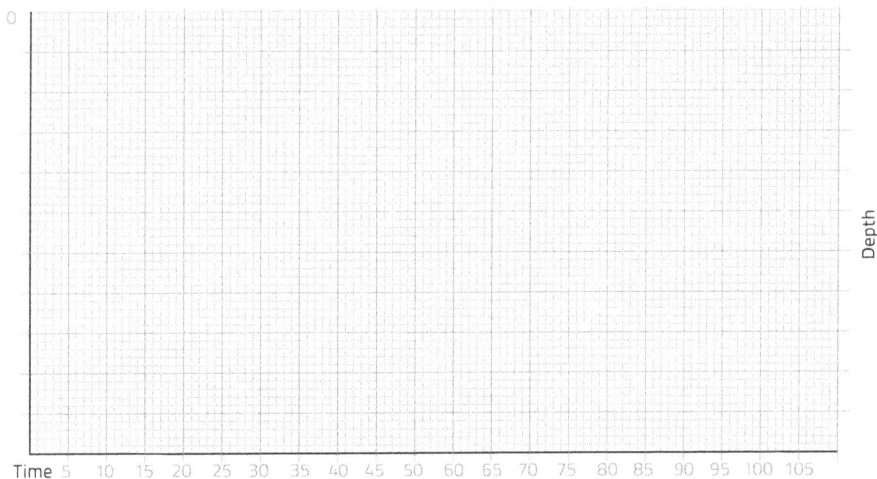

0

Depth

Time   5   10   15   20   25   30   35   40   45   50   55   60   65   70   75   80   85   90   95   100   105

Summary

Description/Sketch

DIVED UP

Water Speed Slack / Slow / Steady / Fast   Temp @ Depth

Sea State   Wind Speed   Temp@ Surface

Kit/Skills Notes

Accumulated Dive Time	:	Milestone?

Verified by

Signature   No.

| DIVE No. | **DIVE LOG** | Date |

Dive Site
Boat/Shore/Inland (circle)

Buddy
Purpose

Boat
Skipper   Port/Launch Site

| Dive No./Day | | Day in Sequence | | Surface Int. | : | Time in | : | out | : |

GAS	Mix	Pressure		Cyl. Size		DIVE TIME	MAX DEPTH
		In	Out				
Bottom							
Travel						mins	m/ft
Deco							

Visibility
m/ft

Stops .... mins @ .... m/ft .... mins @ .... m/ft .... mins @ .... m/ft

Open Circuit ☐ **Semi-Closed** ☐ **Closed Circuit** ☐ **Comp/Tables** ....
Weight .... kg/lbs **OK:** Y / N **(Add/Remove** .... **)**
Suit/Undersuit .... **Gloves** Y / N **Hood** Y / N **Hot / Cold / OK**

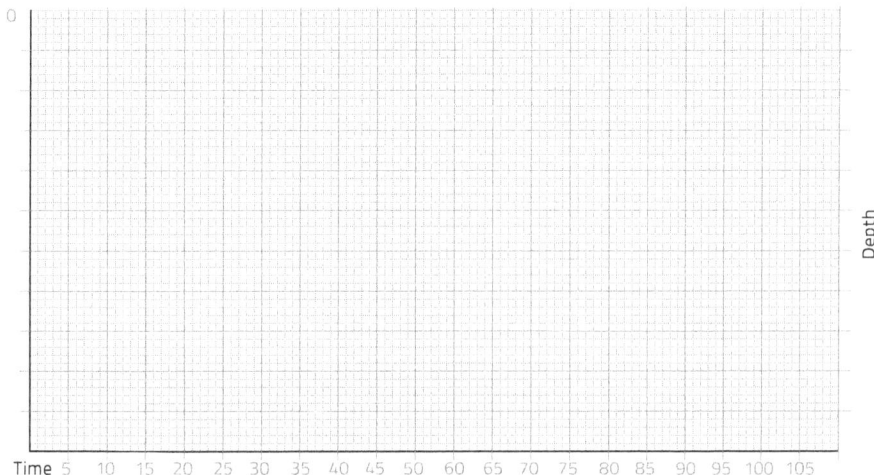

0

Depth

Time 5   10   15   20   25   30   35   40   45   50   55   60   65   70   75   80   85   90   95   100 105

Summary

Description/Sketch

DIVED UP

Water Speed Slack / Slow / Steady / Fast   Temp @ Depth

Sea State   Wind Speed   Temp@ Surface

Kit/Skills Notes

Accumulated Dive Time   :   Milestone?

Verified by

                                        Signature   No.

DIVE No.	**DIVE LOG**	Date

Dive Site — Boat/Shore/Inland (circle)

Buddy — Purpose

Boat — Skipper — Port/Launch Site

| Dive No./Day | Day in Sequence | Surface Int. : | Time in : | out : |

GAS	Mix	Pressure		Cyl. Size	DIVE TIME	MAX DEPTH
		In	Out			
Bottom						
Travel					mins	m/ft
Deco						

Visibility m/ft

Stops .... mins @ .... m/ft .... mins @ .... m/ft .... mins @ .... m/ft

Open Circuit ☐ Semi-Closed ☐ Closed Circuit ☐ Comp/Tables ....

Weight .... kg/lbs **OK:** Y / N (**Add/Remove** ....)

Suit/Undersuit .... **Gloves** Y / N **Hood** Y / N **Hot / Cold / OK**

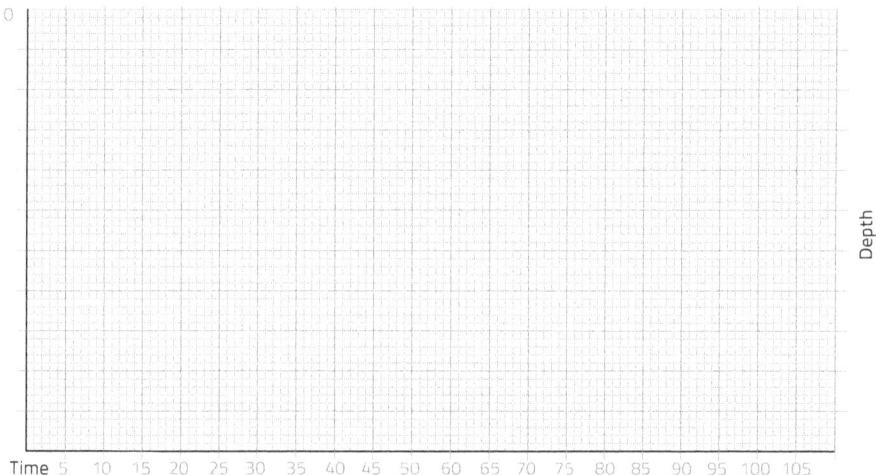

0

Depth

Time 5 10 15 20 25 30 35 40 45 50 60 65 70 75 80 85 90 95 100 105

Summary

Description/Sketch

DIVED UP

Water Speed   Slack / Slow / Steady / Fast   Temp @ Depth

Sea State   Wind Speed   Temp@ Surface

Kit/Skills Notes

Accumulated Dive Time   :   Milestone?

Verified by

                              Signature   No.

DIVE LOG

DIVE No.

Date

Dive Site   Boat/Shore/Inland (circle)

Buddy   Purpose

Boat   Skipper   Port/Launch Site

Dive No./Day | Day in Sequence | Surface Int. : | Time in : out :

GAS	Mix	Pressure		Cyl. Size
		In	Out	
Bottom				
Travel				
Deco				

DIVE TIME

mins

MAX DEPTH

m/ft

Visibility

m/ft

Stops .... mins @ .... m/ft   .... mins @ .... m/ft   .... mins @ .... m/ft

Open Circuit ☐   **Semi-Closed** ☐   **Closed Circuit** ☐   **Comp/Tables** ....

Weight ....kg/lbs **OK:** Y / N **(Add/Remove** ....**)**

Suit/Undersuit .... **Gloves** Y / N **Hood** Y / N **Hot / Cold / OK**

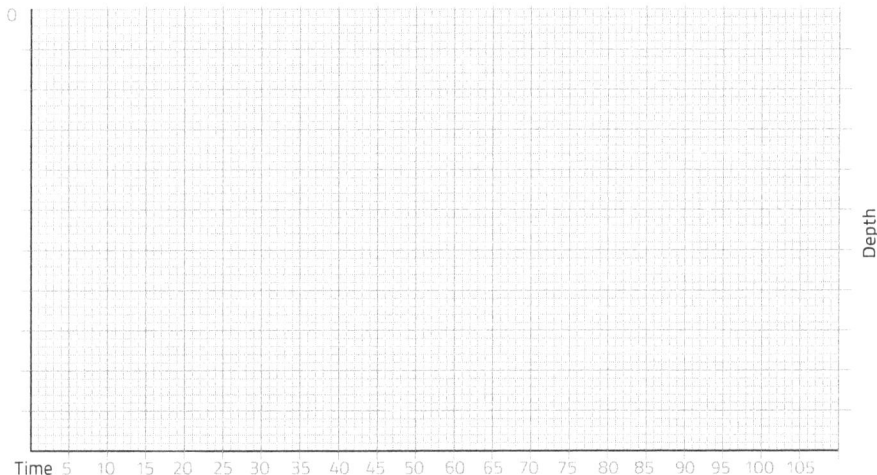

0

Depth

Time 5 10 15 20 25 30 35 40 45 50 60 65 70 75 80 85 90 95 100 105

Summary

Description/Sketch

DIVED UP

Water Speed Slack / Slow / Steady / Fast   Temp @ Depth

Sea State   Wind Speed   Temp@ Surface

Kit/Skills Notes

Accumulated Dive Time   :   Milestone?

Verified by

Signature   No.

DIVE No.	**DIVE LOG**	Date

Dive Site   Boat/Shore/Inland (circle)

Buddy   Purpose

Boat   Skipper   Port/Launch Site

Dive No./Day		Day in Sequence		Surface Int.	:	Time in	:	out	:

GAS	Mix	Pressure		Cyl. Size	**DIVE TIME**	**MAX DEPTH**
		In	Out			
Bottom						
Travel					mins	m/ft
Deco						

Visibility

m/ft

Stops .... mins @ .... m/ft   .... mins @ .... m/ft   .... mins @ .... m/ft

Open Circuit   **Semi-Closed**   **Closed Circuit**   **Comp/Tables** ....
Weight ....kg/lbs **OK:** Y / N   **(Add/Remove**...............**)**
Suit/Undersuit .... **Gloves** Y / N   **Hood** Y / N   **Hot / Cold / OK**

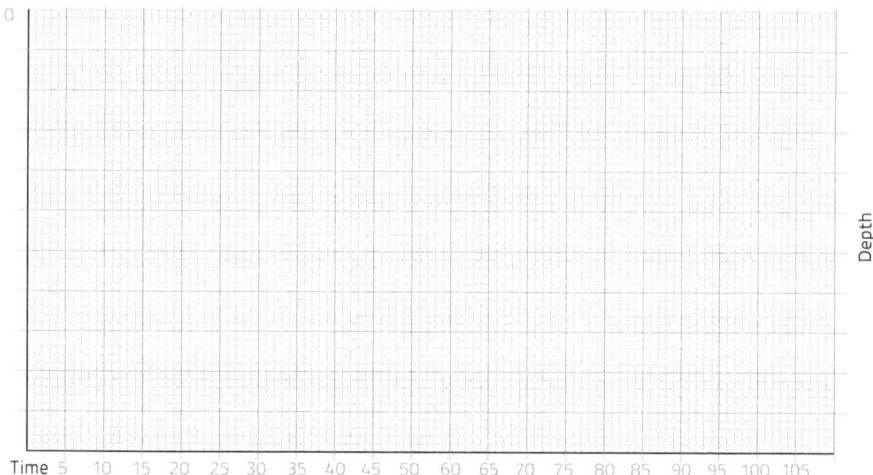

0

Depth

Time 5   10   15   20   25   30   35   40   45   50   60   65   70   75   80   85   90   95   100 105

Summary

Description/Sketch

DIVED UP

Water Speed Slack / Slow / Steady / Fast   Temp @ Depth

Sea State   Wind Speed   Temp@ Surface

Kit/Skills Notes

Accumulated Dive Time   :   Milestone?

Verified by

Signature   No.

DIVE No.   **DIVE LOG**   **Date**

Dive Site   Boat/Shore/Inland (circle)

Buddy   Purpose

Boat   Skipper   Port/Launch Site

Dive No./Day		Day in Sequence		Surface Int.	:	Time in	:	out	:

GAS	Mix	Pressure		Cyl. Size
		In	Out	
Bottom				
Travel				
Deco				

DIVE TIME	**MAX DEPTH**
mins	m/ft

Visibility   m/ft

Stops .... mins @ .... m/ft   .... mins @ .... m/ft   .... mins @ .... m/ft

Open Circuit ☐   Semi-Closed ☐   Closed Circuit ☐   Comp/Tables ....
Weight .... kg/lbs   **OK:** Y / N   **(Add/Remove** .... **)**
Suit/Undersuit .... **Gloves** Y / N   **Hood** Y / N   **Hot / Cold / OK**

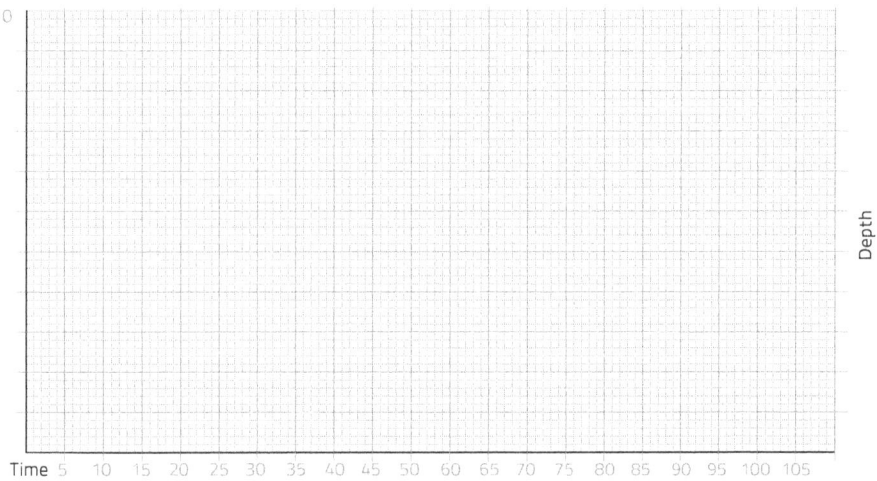

Time   5   10   15   20   25   30   35   40   45   50   60   65   70   75   80   85   90   95   100   105   Depth

Summary

Description/Sketch

DIVED UP

Water Speed Slack / Slow / Steady / Fast		Temp @ Depth
Sea State	Wind Speed	Temp@ Surface

Kit/Skills Notes

Accumulated Dive Time :	Milestone?

Verified by

Signature   No.

DIVE LOG

DIVE No.

Date

Dive Site   Boat/Shore/Inland (circle)

Buddy   Purpose

Boat   Skipper   Port/Launch Site

Dive No./Day   Day in Sequence   Surface Int.   :   Time in   :   out   :

GAS	Mix	Pressure		Cyl. Size
		In	Out	
Bottom				
Travel				
Deco				

DIVE TIME	MAX DEPTH
mins	m/ft

Visibility
m/ft

Stops .... mins @ .... m/ft .... mins @ .... m/ft .... mins @ .... m/ft

Open Circuit ☐   Semi-Closed ☐   Closed Circuit ☐   **Comp/Tables** ....

Weight ....kg/lbs **OK:** Y / N **(Add/Remove** ....**)**

Suit/Undersuit .... **Gloves** Y / N   **Hood** Y / N   **Hot / Cold / OK**

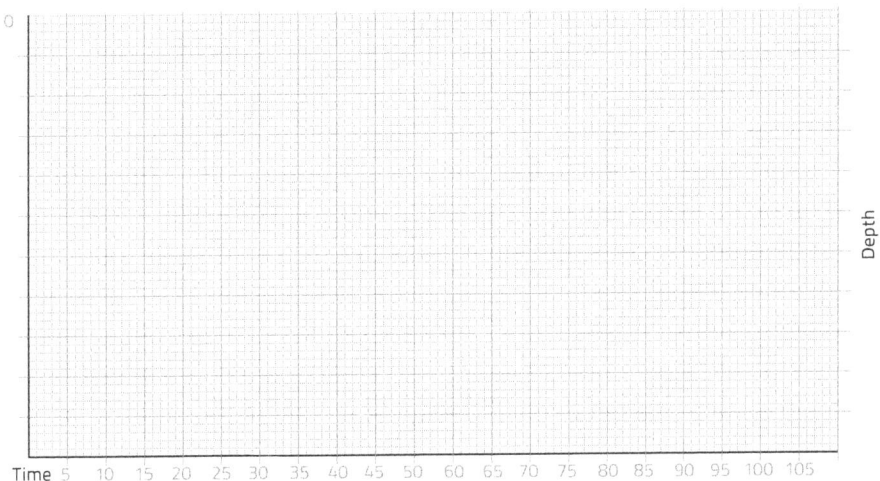

Depth

Time 5   10   15   20   25   30   35   40   45   50   60   65   70   75   80   85   90   95   100 105

Summary

Description/Sketch

DIVED UP

Water Speed   Slack / Slow / Steady / Fast   Temp @ Depth

Sea State   Wind Speed   Temp@ Surface

Kit/Skills Notes

Accumulated Dive Time   :   Milestone?

Verified by

Signature   No.

DIVE No. **DIVE LOG** **Date**

Dive Site Boat/Shore/Inland (circle)

Buddy Purpose

Boat Skipper Port/Launch Site

| Dive No./Day | | Day in Sequence | | Surface Int. | : | Time in | : | out | : |

GAS	Mix	Pressure		Cyl. Size
		In	Out	
Bottom				
Travel				
Deco				

DIVE TIME _____ mins

MAX DEPTH _____ m/ft

Visibility _____ m/ft

Stops .... mins @ .... m/ft .... mins @ .... m/ft .... mins @ .... m/ft

Open Circuit ☐ **Semi-Closed** ☐ **Closed Circuit** ☐ **Comp/Tables** ....

Weight .... kg/lbs **OK:** Y / N **(Add/Remove** .... **)**

Suit/Undersuit .... **Gloves** Y / N **Hood** Y / N **Hot / Cold / OK**

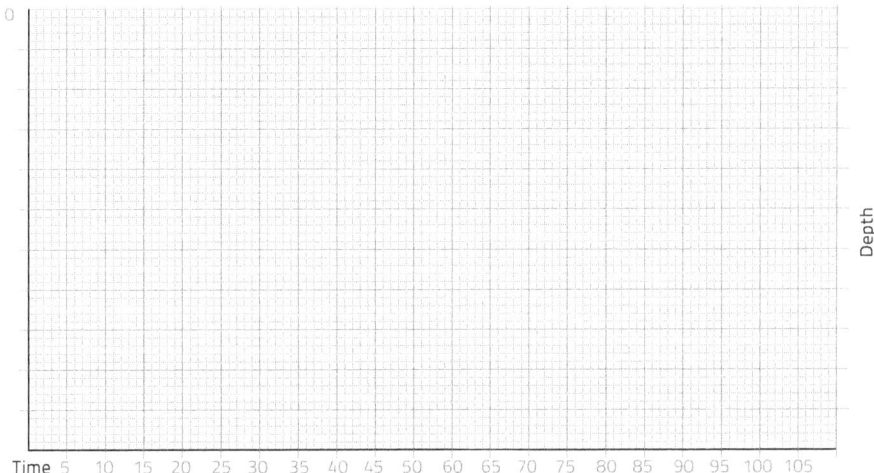

0

Depth

Time 5 10 15 20 25 30 35 40 45 50 55 60 65 70 75 80 85 90 95 100 105

Summary

Description/Sketch

DIVED UP

Water Speed   Slack / Slow / Steady / Fast   Temp @ Depth

Sea State   Wind Speed   Temp@ Surface

Kit/Skills Notes

Accumulated Dive Time   :   Milestone?

Verified by

                              Signature   No.

DIVE No.	DIVE LOG	Date

Dive Site | Boat/Shore/Inland (circle)

Buddy | Purpose

Boat | Skipper | Port/Launch Site

| Dive No./Day | | Day in Sequence | | Surface Int. | : | Time in | : | out | : |

GAS	Mix	Pressure		Cyl. Size	DIVE TIME	MAX DEPTH
		In	Out			
Bottom						
Travel						
Deco					mins	m/ft

Visibility m/ft

Stops .... mins @ .... m/ft .... mins @ .... m/ft .... mins @ .... m/ft

Open Circuit ☐ Semi-Closed ☐ Closed Circuit ☐ Comp/Tables ....

Weight ....kg/lbs **OK:** Y / N **(Add/Remove** ....**)**

Suit/Undersuit ....**Gloves** Y / N **Hood** Y / N **Hot / Cold / OK**

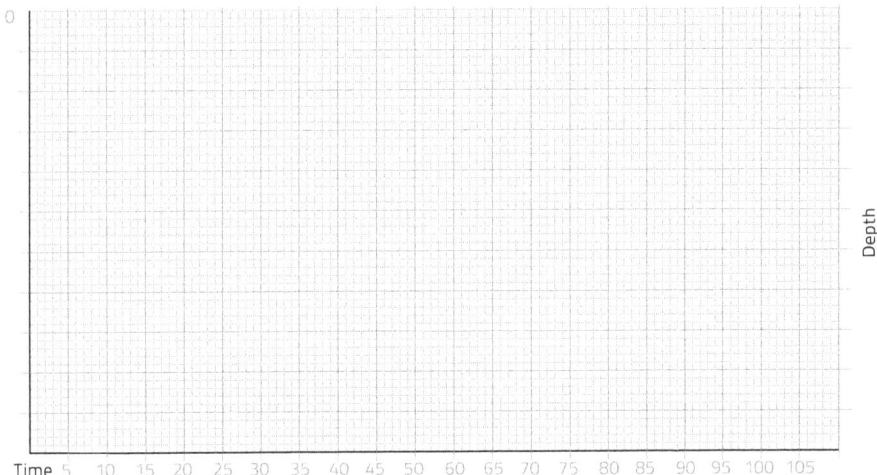

Time 5 10 15 20 25 30 35 40 45 50 60 65 70 75 80 85 90 95 100 105

Depth

Summary

Description/Sketch

DIVED UP

Water Speed Slack / Slow / Steady / Fast   Temp @ Depth

Sea State   Wind Speed   Temp@ Surface

Kit/Skills Notes

Accumulated Dive Time   :   Milestone?

Verified by

Signature   No.

DIVE LOG

DIVE No.

Date

Dive Site

Boat/Shore/Inland (circle)

Buddy

Purpose

Boat

Skipper

Port/Launch Site

Dive No./Day		Day in Sequence		Surface Int.	:	Time in	:	out	:

GAS	Mix	Pressure		Cyl. Size
		In	Out	
Bottom				
Travel				
Deco				

DIVE TIME

mins

MAX DEPTH

m/ft

Visibility

m/ft

Stops .... mins @ .... m/ft .... mins @ .... m/ft .... mins @ .... m/ft

Open Circuit ☐ **Semi-Closed** ☐ **Closed Circuit** ☐ **Comp/Tables** ....

Weight ....kg/lbs **OK:** Y / N **(Add/Remove** .... **)**

Suit/Undersuit .... **Gloves** Y / N **Hood** Y / N **Hot / Cold / OK**

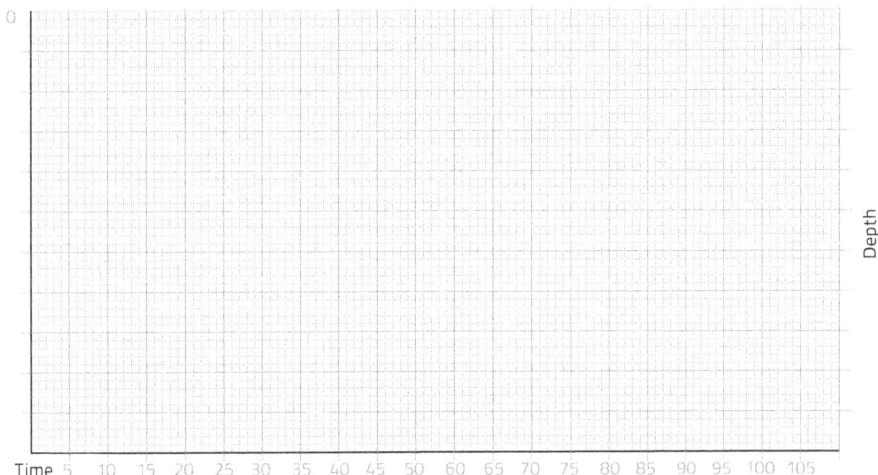

0

Depth

Time 5 10 15 20 25 30 35 40 45 50 60 65 70 75 80 85 90 95 100 105

Summary

Description/Sketch

DIVED UP

Water Speed	Slack / Slow / Steady / Fast		Temp @ Depth
Sea State		Wind Speed	Temp @ Surface

Kit/Skills Notes

Accumulated Dive Time	:	Milestone?

Verified by

Signature   No.

| DIVE No. | | DIVE LOG | | Date |

Dive Site

Boat/Shore/Inland (circle)

Buddy   Purpose

Boat   Skipper   Port/Launch Site

| Dive No./Day | | Day in Sequence | | Surface Int. | : | Time in | : | out | : |

GAS	Mix	Pressure		Cyl. Size
		In	Out	
Bottom				
Travel				
Deco				

DIVE TIME	MAX DEPTH
mins	m/ft

Visibility

m/ft

Stops .... mins @ .... m/ft   .... mins @ .... m/ft   .... mins @ .... m/ft

Open Circuit ☐   **Semi-Closed** ☐   **Closed Circuit** ☐   **Comp/Tables** ....

Weight .... kg/lbs   **OK:** Y / N   **(Add/Remove** .... **)**

Suit/Undersuit .... **Gloves** Y / N   **Hood** Y / N   **Hot / Cold / OK**

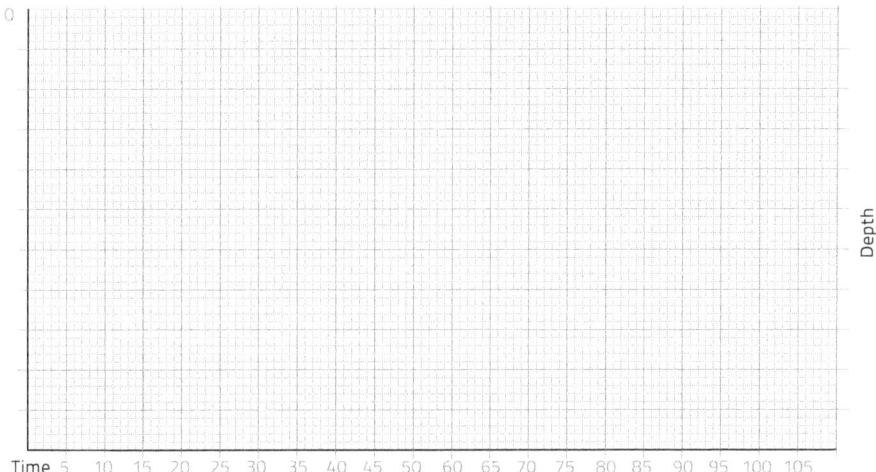

Depth

Time 5   10   15   20   25   30   35   40   45   50   60   65   70   75   80   85   90   95   100   105

Summary

Description/Sketch

DIVED UP

Water Speed Slack / Slow / Steady / Fast   Temp @ Depth

Sea State   Wind Speed   Temp@ Surface

Kit/Skills Notes

Accumulated Dive Time   :   Milestone?

Verified by

Signature   No.

| DIVE No. | DIVE LOG | Date |

Dive Site
Boat/Shore/Inland (circle)

Buddy   Purpose

Boat   Skipper   Port/Launch Site

| Dive No./Day | | Day in Sequence | | Surface Int. | : | Time in | : | out | : |

GAS	Mix	Pressure		Cyl. Size
		In	Out	
Bottom				
Travel				
Deco				

DIVE TIME

mins

MAX DEPTH

m/ft

Visibility

m/ft

Stops .... mins @ .... m/ft   .... mins @ .... m/ft   .... mins @ .... m/ft

Open Circuit ☐   Semi-Closed ☐   Closed Circuit ☐   Comp/Tables ....
Weight ....kg/lbs   **OK:** Y / N   **(Add/Remove** ....**)**
Suit/Undersuit ....**Gloves** Y / N   **Hood** Y / N   **Hot / Cold / OK**

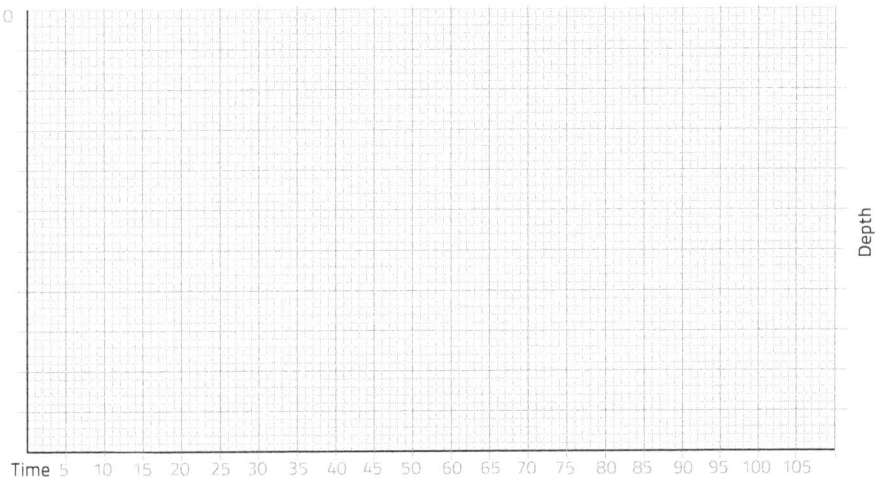

0

Depth

Time 5 10 15 20 25 30 35 40 45 50 60 65 70 75 80 85 90 95 100 105

Summary

Description/Sketch

DIVED UP

Water Speed Slack / Slow / Steady / Fast   Temp @ Depth

Sea State   Wind Speed   Temp@ Surface

Kit/Skills Notes

Accumulated Dive Time   :   Milestone?

Verified by

                              Signature   No.

DIVE No.	**DIVE LOG**	Date

Dive Site	Boat/Shore/Inland (circle)

Buddy	Purpose

Boat	Skipper	Port/Launch Site

Dive No./Day		Day in Sequence		Surface Int.	:	Time in	:	out	:

GAS	Mix	Pressure In	Pressure Out	Cyl. Size
Bottom				
Travel				
Deco				

DIVE TIME	MAX DEPTH
mins	m/ft

Visibility
m/ft

Stops .... mins @ .... m/ft .... mins @ .... m/ft .... mins @ .... m/ft

Open Circuit	Semi-Closed	Closed Circuit	Comp/Tables ....

Weight ....kg/lbs **OK:** Y / N **(Add/Remove** ....**)**

Suit/Undersuit .... **Gloves** Y / N **Hood** Y / N **Hot / Cold / OK**

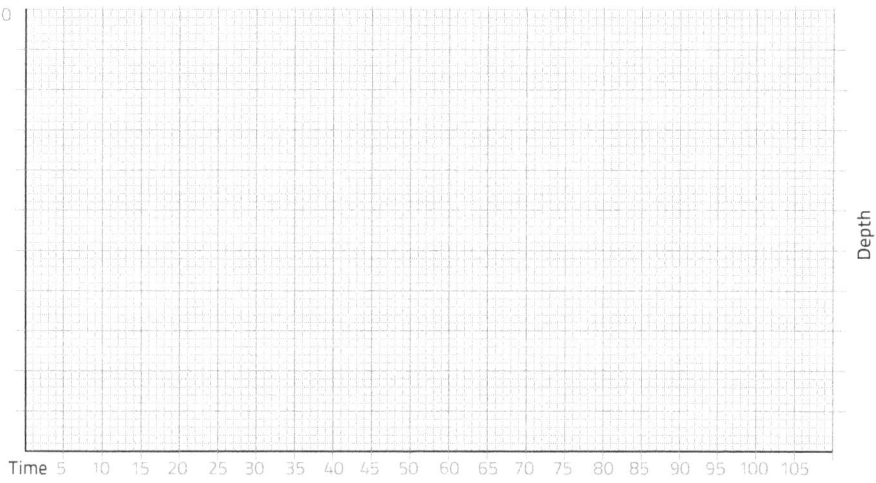

Time 5 10 15 20 25 30 35 40 45 50 55 60 65 70 75 80 85 90 95 100 105

Depth

Summary

Description/Sketch

(blank ruled lines)

DIVED UP

Water Speed Slack / Slow / Steady / Fast		Temp @ Depth
Sea State	Wind Speed	Temp@ Surface

Kit/Skills Notes

Accumulated Dive Time :	Milestone?

Verified by

Signature   No.

DIVE LOG

DIVE No.

Date

Dive Site   Boat/Shore/Inland (circle)

Buddy   Purpose

Boat   Skipper   Port/Launch Site

Dive No./Day		Day in Sequence		Surface Int.	:	Time in	:	out	:

GAS	Mix	Pressure		Cyl. Size
		In	Out	
Bottom				
Travel				
Deco				

DIVE TIME   mins

MAX DEPTH   m/ft

Visibility   m/ft

Stops .... mins @ .... m/ft   .... mins @ .... m/ft   .... mins @ .... m/ft

Open Circuit   **Semi-Closed**   **Closed Circuit**   **Comp/Tables** ....

Weight .... kg/lbs   **OK:** Y / N   **(Add/Remove** .... **)**

Suit/Undersuit .... **Gloves** Y / N   **Hood** Y / N   **Hot / Cold / OK**

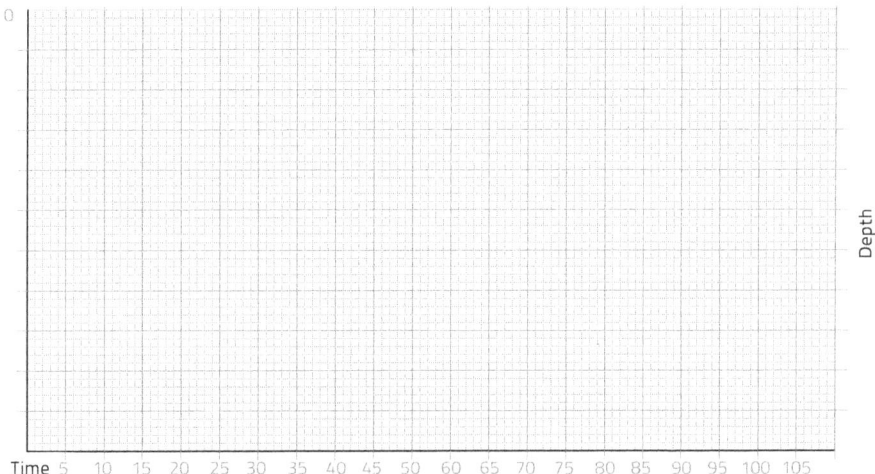

0

Depth

Time   5   10   15   20   25   30   35   40   45   50   55   60   65   70   75   80   85   90   95   100   105

Summary

Description/Sketch

DIVED UP

Water Speed Slack / Slow / Steady / Fast   Temp @ Depth

Sea State   Wind Speed   Temp@ Surface

Kit/Skills Notes

Accumulated Dive Time   :   Milestone?

Verified by

                                             Signature   No.

DIVE LOG

DIVE No.

Date

Dive Site — Boat/Shore/Inland (circle)

Buddy — **Purpose**

Boat — **Skipper** — **Port/Launch Site**

Dive No./Day		Day in Sequence		Surface Int.	:	Time in	:	out	:

GAS	Mix	Pressure		Cyl. Size
		In	Out	
Bottom				
Travel				
Deco				

DIVE TIME _____ mins

MAX DEPTH _____ m/ft

Visibility _____ m/ft

Stops .... mins @ .... m/ft .... mins @ .... m/ft .... mins @ .... m/ft

Open Circuit ☐ Semi-Closed ☐ Closed Circuit ☐ Comp/Tables _____

Weight .... kg/lbs **OK:** Y / N (Add/Remove _____)

Suit/Undersuit .... Gloves Y / N Hood Y / N Hot / Cold / OK

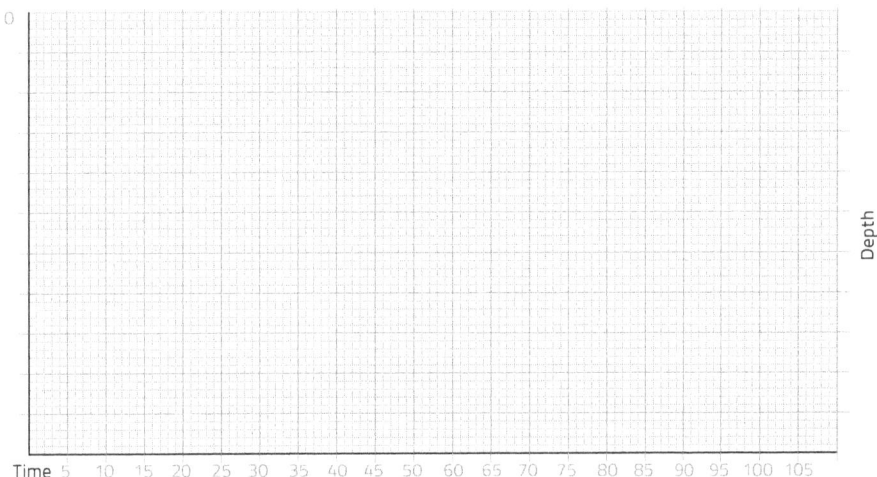

Depth

Time 5 10 15 20 25 30 35 40 45 50 60 65 70 75 80 85 90 95 100 105

Summary

Description/Sketch

DIVED UP

Water Speed   Slack / Slow / Steady / Fast   Temp @ Depth

Sea State   Wind Speed   Temp@ Surface

Kit/Skills Notes

Accumulated Dive Time   :   Milestone?

Verified by

Signature   No.

DIVE LOG

Dive Site   Boat/Shore/Inland (circle)

Buddy   Purpose

Boat   Skipper   Port/Launch Site

| Dive No./Day | | Day in Sequence | | Surface Int. | : | Time in | : | out | : |

GAS	Mix	Pressure		Cyl. Size
		In	Out	
Bottom				
Travel				
Deco				

DIVE TIME   **MAX DEPTH**

mins   m/ft

Visibility

m/ft

Stops .... mins @ .... m/ft .... mins @ .... m/ft .... mins @ .... m/ft

Open Circuit ☐   **Semi-Closed** ☐   **Closed Circuit** ☐   **Comp/Tables** ....

Weight .... kg/lbs   **OK:** Y / N   **(Add/Remove** ....)

Suit/Undersuit ....   **Gloves** Y / N   **Hood** Y / N   **Hot / Cold / OK**

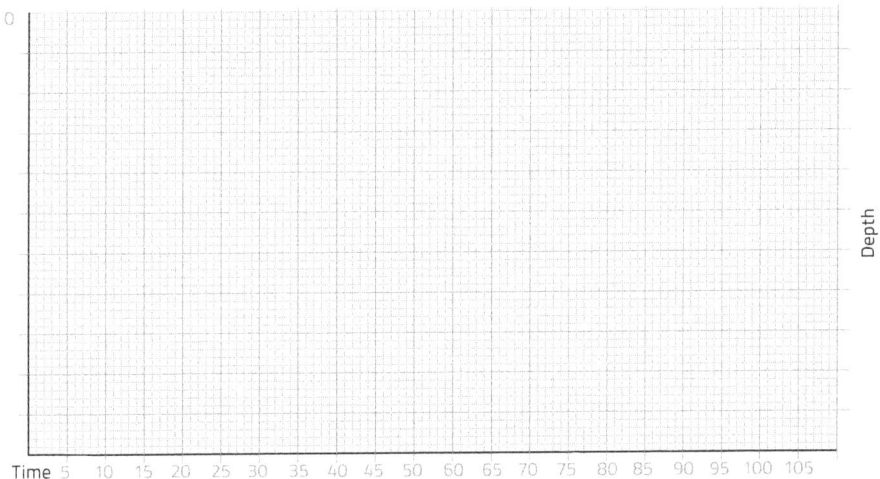

0

Depth

Time 5   10   15   20   25   30   35   40   45   50   55   60   65   70   75   80   85   90   95   100   105

Summary

Description/Sketch

DIVED UP

Water Speed	Slack / Slow / Steady / Fast		Temp @ Depth
Sea State		Wind Speed	Temp@ Surface

Kit/Skills Notes

Accumulated Dive Time	:	Milestone?

Verified by

Signature   No.

DIVE No.	DIVE LOG	Date

Dive Site Boat/Shore/Inland (circle)

Buddy   Purpose

Boat   Skipper   Port/Launch Site

Dive No./Day		Day in Sequence		Surface Int.	:	Time in	:	out	:

GAS	Mix	Pressure		Cyl. Size	DIVE TIME	MAX DEPTH
		In	Out			
Bottom						
Travel					mins	m/ft
Deco						

Visibility
m/ft

Stops .... mins @ .... m/ft   .... mins @ .... m/ft   .... mins @ .... m/ft

Open Circuit ☐   Semi-Closed ☐   Closed Circuit ☐   Comp/Tables ....

Weight .... kg/lbs   **OK:** Y / N   **(Add/Remove** .... **)**

Suit/Undersuit .... **Gloves** Y / N   **Hood** Y / N   **Hot / Cold / OK**

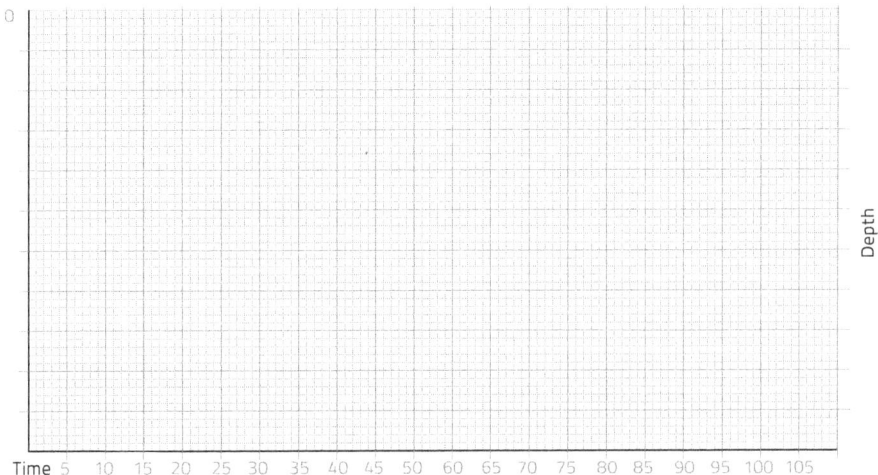

0

Depth

Time 5 10 15 20 25 30 35 40 45 50 60 65 70 75 80 85 90 95 100 105

Summary

Description/Sketch

DIVED UP

Water Speed   Slack / Slow / Steady / Fast   Temp @ Depth
Sea State   Wind Speed   Temp@ Surface

Kit/Skills Notes

Accumulated Dive Time   :   Milestone?

Verified by

                              Signature   No.

DIVE No.	**DIVE LOG**	Date

Dive Site	Boat/Shore/Inland (circle)

Buddy	Purpose

Boat	Skipper	Port/Launch Site

Dive No./Day		Day in Sequence		Surface Int	:	Time in	:	out	:

GAS	Mix	Pressure		Cyl. Size
		In	Out	
Bottom				
Travel				
Deco				

DIVE TIME .... mins

MAX DEPTH .... m/ft

Visibility .... m/ft

Stops .... mins @ .... m/ft .... mins @ .... m/ft .... mins @ .... m/ft

Open Circuit ☐ Semi-Closed ☐ Closed Circuit ☐ Comp/Tables ....
Weight .... kg/lbs **OK:** Y / N **(Add/Remove** ....**)**
Suit/Undersuit ....**Gloves** Y / N **Hood** Y / N **Hot / Cold / OK**

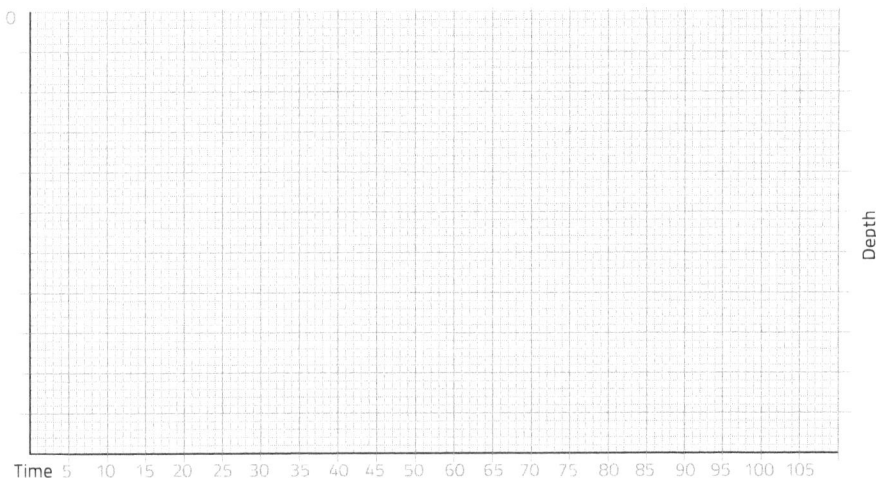

Depth

Time 5 10 15 20 25 30 35 40 45 50 60 65 70 75 80 85 90 95 100 105

Summary

Description/Sketch

DIVED UP

Water Speed Slack / Slow / Steady / Fast   Temp @ Depth

Sea State   Wind Speed   Temp @ Surface

Kit/Skills Notes

Accumulated Dive Time   :   Milestone?

Verified by

                                Signature   No.

DIVE LOG

DIVE No.

Date

Dive Site   Boat/Shore/Inland (circle)

Buddy   Purpose

Boat   Skipper   Port/Launch Site

| Dive No./Day | | Day in Sequence | | Surface Int. | : | Time in | : | out | : |

GAS	Mix	Pressure		Cyl. Size
		In	Out	
Bottom				
Travel				
Deco				

DIVE TIME
mins

MAX DEPTH
m/ft

Visibility
m/ft

Stops .... mins @ .... m/ft   .... mins @ .... m/ft   .... mins @ .... m/ft

Open Circuit ☐   Semi-Closed ☐   Closed Circuit ☐   Comp/Tables ....

Weight ....kg/lbs **OK:** Y / N **(Add/Remove** .... **)**

Suit/Undersuit .... **Gloves** Y / N **Hood** Y / N **Hot / Cold / OK**

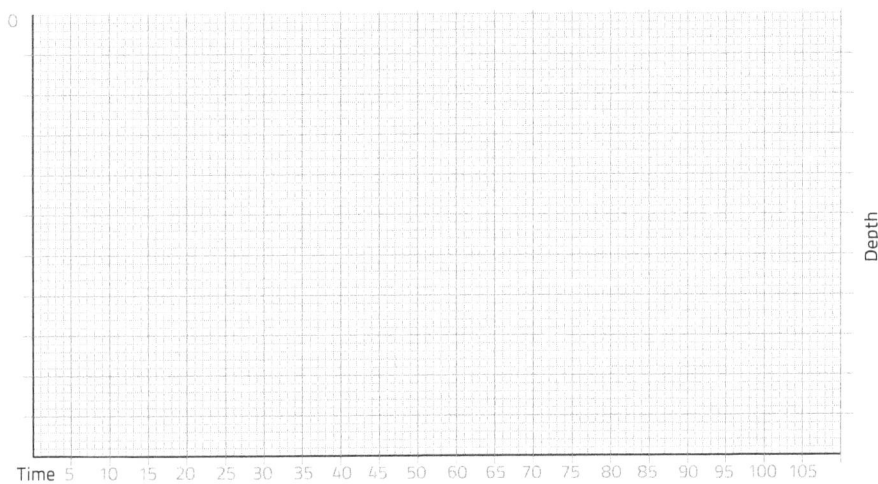

Depth

Time 5   10   15   20   25   30   35   40   45   50   60   65   70   75   80   85   90   95   100   105

Summary

Description/Sketch

Water Speed Slack / Slow / Steady / Fast   Temp @ Depth

Sea State   Wind Speed   Temp@ Surface

Kit/Skills Notes

Accumulated Dive Time   :   Milestone?

Verified by

Signature   No.

DIVE No.	**DIVE LOG**	Date

Dive Site   Boat/Shore/Inland (circle)

Buddy   Purpose

Boat   Skipper   Port/Launch Site

Dive No./Day		Day in Sequence		Surface Int.	:	Time in	:	out	:

GAS	Mix	Pressure		Cyl. Size	**DIVE TIME**	**MAX DEPTH**
		In	Out			
Bottom						
Travel					mins	m/ft
Deco					Visibility	
						m/ft

Stops .... mins @ .... m/ft .... mins @ .... m/ft .... mins @ .... m/ft

Open Circuit ☐ **Semi-Closed** ☐ **Closed Circuit** ☐ **Comp/Tables** ....

Weight .... kg/lbs **OK:** Y / N **(Add/Remove** .... **)**

Suit/Undersuit .... **Gloves** Y / N **Hood** Y / N **Hot / Cold / OK**

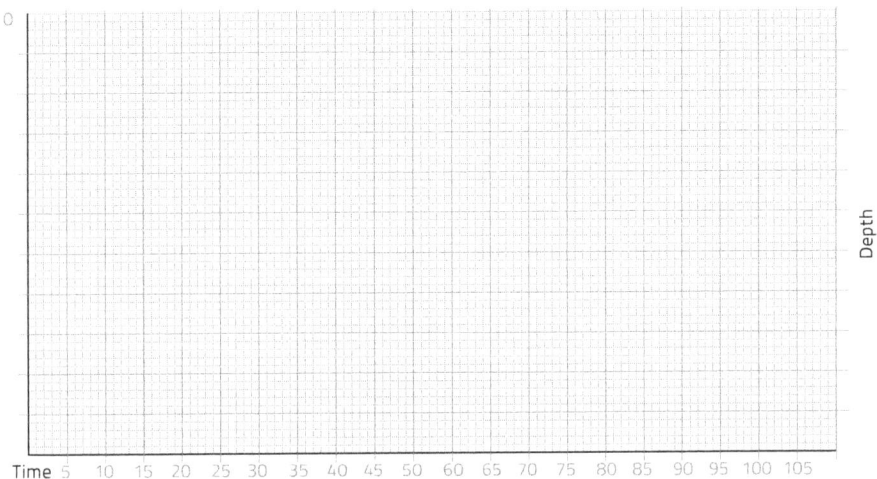

Depth

Time 5 10 15 20 25 30 35 40 45 50 60 65 70 75 80 85 90 95 100 105

Summary

Description/Sketch

DIVED UP

Water Speed   Slack / Slow / Steady / Fast   Temp @ Depth

Sea State   Wind Speed   Temp@ Surface

Kit/Skills Notes

Accumulated Dive Time   :   Milestone?

Verified by

                              Signature   No.

DIVE No.	DIVE LOG	Date

Dive Site   Boat/Shore/Inland (circle)

Buddy   Purpose

Boat   Skipper   Port/Launch Site

Dive No./Day		Day in Sequence		Surface Int.	:	Time in	:	out	:

GAS	Mix	Pressure		Cyl. Size
		In	Out	
Bottom				
Travel				
Deco				

DIVE TIME   **MAX DEPTH**

mins   m/ft

Visibility

m/ft

Stops .... mins @ .... m/ft .... mins @ .... m/ft .... mins @ .... m/ft

Open Circuit ☐   **Semi-Closed** ☐   **Closed Circuit** ☐   **Comp/Tables** ....

Weight ....kg/lbs   **OK:** Y / N   **(Add/Remove** ....)

Suit/Undersuit ....**Gloves** Y / N   **Hood** Y / N   **Hot / Cold / OK**

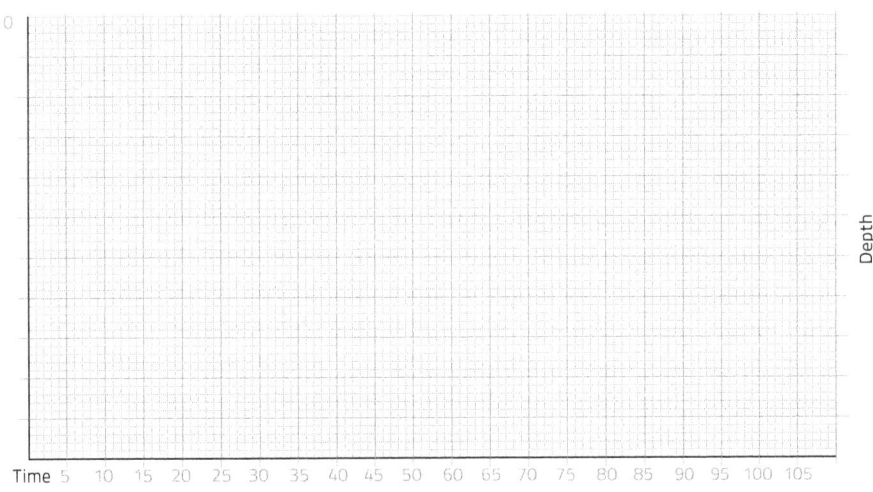

Time 5   10   15   20   25   30   35   40   45   50   55   60   65   70   75   80   85   90   95   100   105

Depth

Summary

Description/Sketch

DIVED UP

| Water Speed | Slack / Slow / Steady / Fast | | Temp @ Depth |
| Sea State | | Wind Speed | Temp@ Surface |

Kit/Skills Notes

| Accumulated Dive Time | : | Milestone? |

Verified by

Signature   No.

DIVE LOG

DIVE No.		Date

Dive Site — Boat/Shore/Inland (circle)

Buddy — Purpose

Boat — Skipper — Port/Launch Site

Dive No./Day		Day in Sequence		Surface Int.	:	Time in	:	out	:

GAS	Mix	Pressure		Cyl. Size
		In	Out	
Bottom				
Travel				
Deco				

DIVE TIME .... mins

MAX DEPTH .... m/ft

Visibility .... m/ft

Stops .... mins @ .... m/ft .... mins @ .... m/ft .... mins @ .... m/ft

Open Circuit ☐ Semi-Closed ☐ Closed Circuit ☐ Comp/Tables ....

Weight .... kg/lbs **OK:** Y / N (Add/Remove ....)

Suit/Undersuit .... **Gloves** Y / N **Hood** Y / N **Hot / Cold / OK**

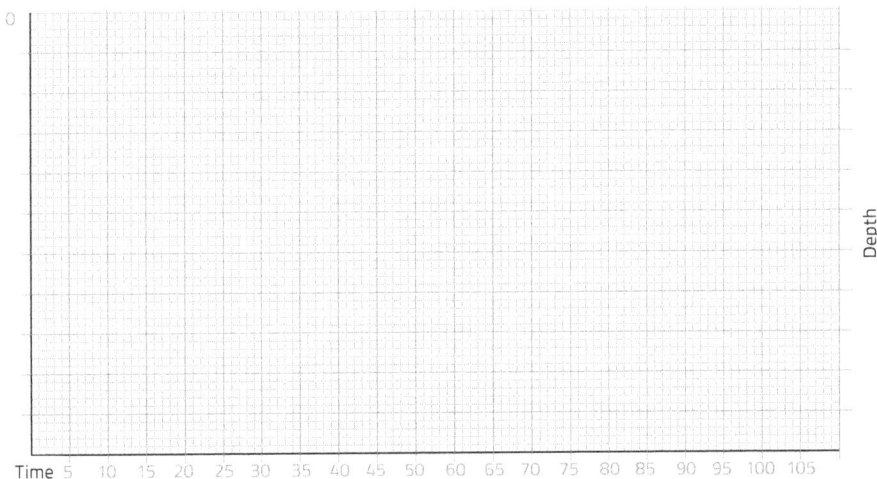

Depth

Time 5   10   15   20   25   30   35   40   45   50   55   60   65   70   75   80   85   90   95   100   105

Summary

Description/Sketch

DIVED UP

Water Speed Slack / Slow / Steady / Fast   Temp @ Depth

Sea State   Wind Speed   Temp@ Surface

Kit/Skills Notes

Accumulated Dive Time   :   Milestone?

Verified by

                                        Signature   No.

| DIVE No. | **DIVE LOG** | Date |

Dive Site
Boat/Shore/Inland (circle)

Buddy
Purpose

Boat
Skipper   Port/Launch Site

| Dive No./Day | | Day in Sequence | | Surface Int. | : | Time in | : | out | : |

GAS	Mix	Pressure		Cyl. Size
		In	Out	
Bottom				
Travel				
Deco				

DIVE TIME
mins

MAX DEPTH
m/ft

Visibility
m/ft

Stops .... mins @ .... m/ft   .... mins @ .... m/ft   .... mins @ .... m/ft

Open Circuit ☐   Semi-Closed ☐   Closed Circuit ☐   Comp/Tables ....

Weight .... kg/lbs **OK:** Y / N   (Add/Remove ....)

Suit/Undersuit .... **Gloves** Y / N   **Hood** Y / N   **Hot / Cold / OK**

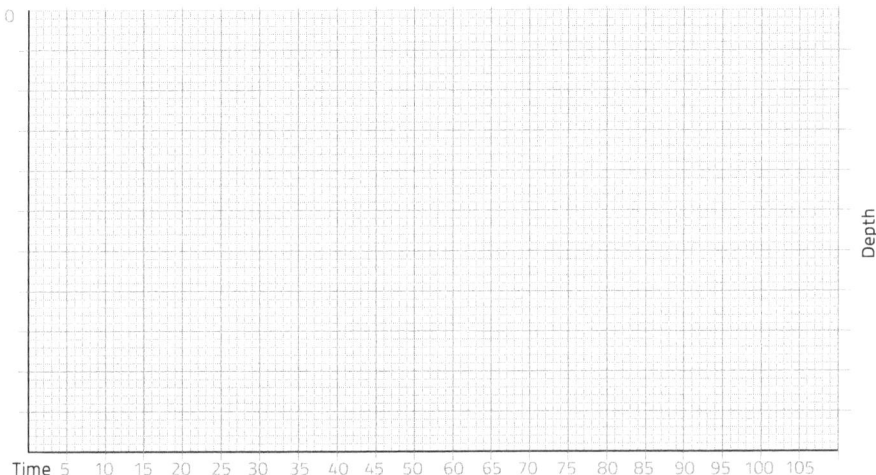

0

Depth

Time 5   10   15   20   25   30   35   40   45   50   55   60   65   70   75   80   85   90   95   100   105

Summary

Description/Sketch

DIVED UP

Water Speed Slack / Slow / Steady / Fast   Temp @ Depth

Sea State   Wind Speed   Temp@ Surface

Kit/Skills Notes

Accumulated Dive Time   :   Milestone?

Verified by

Signature   No.

DIVE LOG

DIVE No.

Date

Dive Site   Boat/Shore/Inland (circle)

Buddy   Purpose

Boat   Skipper   Port/Launch Site

Dive No./Day   Day in Sequence   Surface Int.   :   Time in   :   out   :

GAS	Mix	Pressure		Cyl. Size
		In	Out	
Bottom				
Travel				
Deco				

DIVE TIME   mins

MAX DEPTH   m/ft

Visibility   m/ft

Stops .... mins @ .... m/ft   .... mins @ .... m/ft   .... mins @ .... m/ft

Open Circuit   **Semi-Closed**   **Closed Circuit**   **Comp/Tables** ....

Weight ....kg/lbs   **OK:** Y / N   **(Add/Remove** ....)

Suit/Undersuit ....   **Gloves** Y / N   **Hood** Y / N   **Hot / Cold / OK**

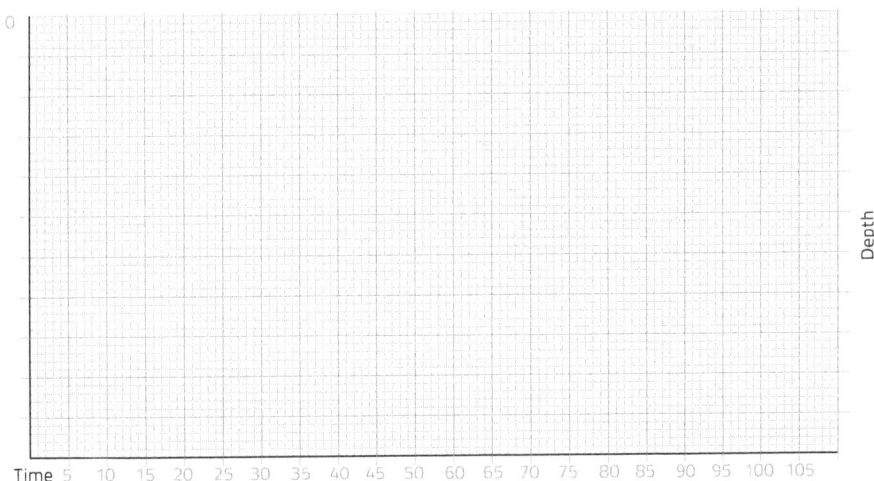

0

Depth

Time   5   10   15   20   25   30   35   40   45   50   55   60   65   70   75   80   85   90   95   100   105

Summary

Description/Sketch

DIVED UP

Water Speed Slack / Slow / Steady / Fast   Temp @ Depth

Sea State   Wind Speed   Temp@ Surface

Kit/Skills Notes

Accumulated Dive Time   :   Milestone?

Verified by

                                        Signature   No.

DIVE LOG

DIVE No.

Date

Dive Site   Boat/Shore/Inland (circle)

Buddy   Purpose

Boat   Skipper   Port/Launch Site

| Dive No./Day | | Day in Sequence | | Surface Int. | : | Time in | : | out | : |

GAS	Mix	Pressure		Cyl. Size
		In	Out	
Bottom				
Travel				
Deco				

DIVE TIME

mins

MAX DEPTH

m/ft

Visibility

m/ft

Stops .... mins @ .... m/ft   .... mins @ .... m/ft   .... mins @ .... m/ft

Open Circuit ☐   Semi-Closed ☐   Closed Circuit ☐   Comp/Tables ....

Weight .... kg/lbs   **OK:** Y / N   (Add/Remove ....)

Suit/Undersuit .... **Gloves** Y / N   **Hood** Y / N   **Hot / Cold / OK**

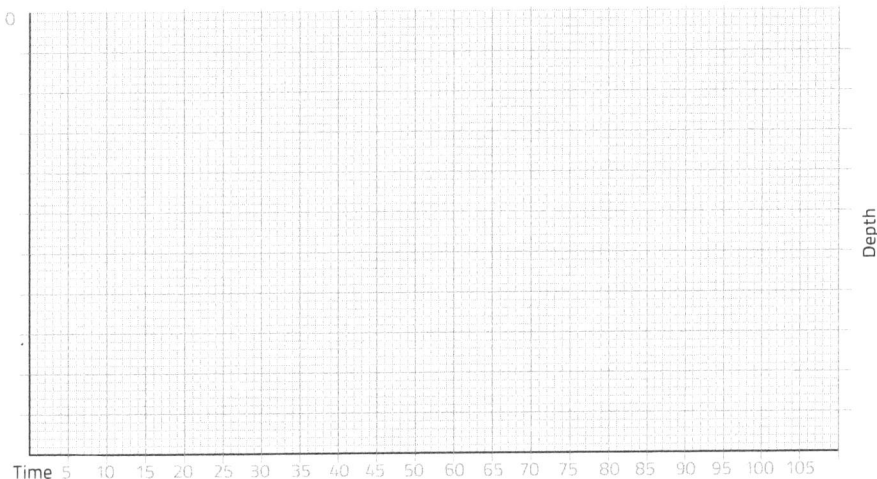

Depth

Time 5   10   15   20   25   30   35   40   45   50   60   65   70   75   80   85   90   95   100   105

Summary

Description/Sketch

Water Speed Slack / Slow / Steady / Fast   Temp @ Depth

Sea State   Wind Speed   Temp@ Surface

Kit/Skills Notes

Accumulated Dive Time   :   Milestone?

Verified by

                                           Signature   No.

DIVE LOG

DIVE No.		Date

Dive Site — Boat/Shore/Inland (circle)

Buddy — Purpose

Boat — Skipper — Port/Launch Site

Dive No./Day		Day in Sequence		Surface Int.	:	Time in	:	out	:

GAS	Mix	Pressure		Cyl. Size
		In	Out	
Bottom				
Travel				
Deco				

DIVE TIME .... mins

MAX DEPTH .... m/ft

Visibility .... m/ft

Stops .... mins @ .... m/ft .... mins @ .... m/ft .... mins @ .... m/ft

Open Circuit ☐ **Semi-Closed** ☐ **Closed Circuit** ☐ **Comp/Tables** ....

Weight .... kg/lbs **OK:** Y / N **(Add/Remove** .... **)**

Suit/Undersuit .... **Gloves** Y / N **Hood** Y / N **Hot / Cold / OK**

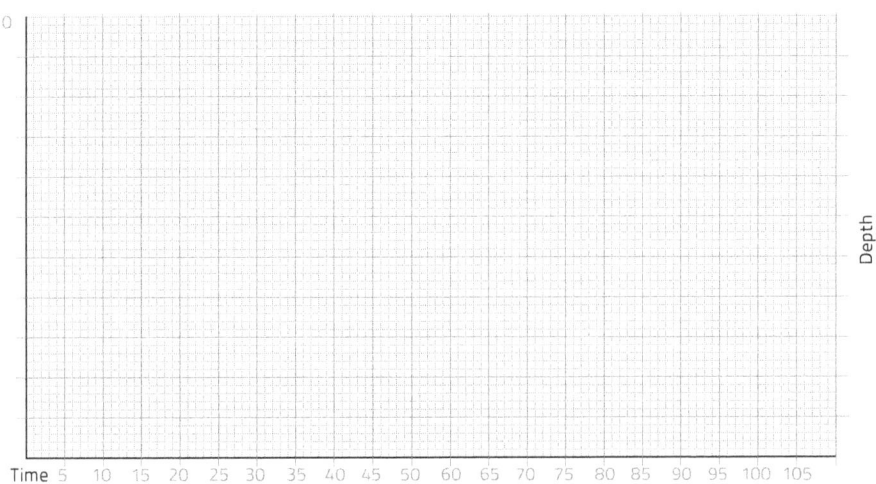

0

Time 5 10 15 20 25 30 35 40 45 50 55 60 65 70 75 80 85 90 95 100 105

Depth

Summary

Description/Sketch

DIVED UP

Water Speed Slack / Slow / Steady / Fast		Temp @ Depth
Sea State	Wind Speed	Temp@ Surface

Kit/Skills Notes

Accumulated Dive Time	:	Milestone?

Verified by

Signature   No.

DIVE LOG

DIVE No.

Date

Dive Site

Boat/Shore/Inland (circle)

Buddy

Purpose

Boat

Skipper

Port/Launch Site

Dive No./Day | Day in Sequence | Surface Int: : | Time in : | out :

GAS	Mix	Pressure		Cyl. Size
		In	Out	
Bottom				
Travel				
Deco				

DIVE TIME

mins

MAX DEPTH

m/ft

Visibility

m/ft

Stops .... mins @ .... m/ft .... mins @ .... m/ft .... mins @ .... m/ft

Open Circuit ☐   Semi-Closed ☐   Closed Circuit ☐   **Comp/Tables** ....

Weight ....kg/lbs   **OK:** Y / N   **(Add/Remove** ....**)**

Suit/Undersuit ....**Gloves** Y / N   **Hood** Y / N   Hot / Cold / OK

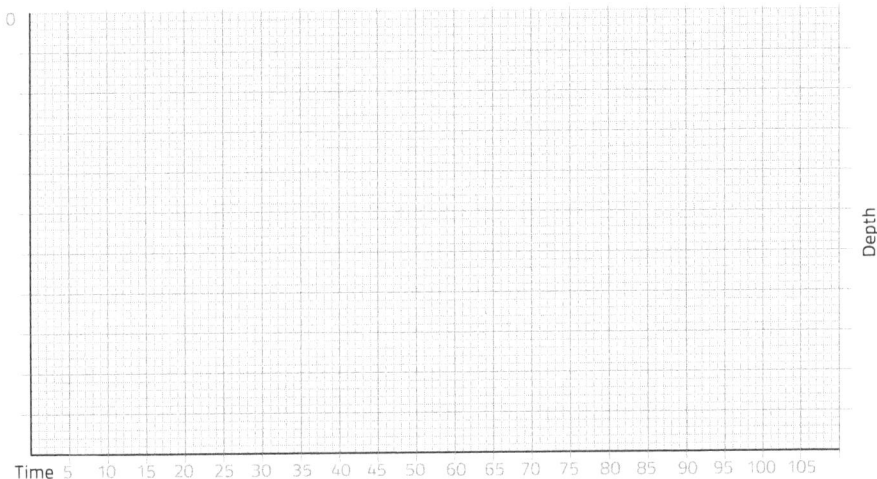

0

Depth

Time 5   10   15   20   25   30   35   40   45   50   60   65   70   75   80   85   90   95   100 105

Summary

Description/Sketch

DIVED UP

Water Speed   Slack / Slow / Steady / Fast   Temp @ Depth

Sea State   Wind Speed   Temp@ Surface

Kit/Skills Notes

Accumulated Dive Time   :   Milestone?

Verified by

Signature   No.

DIVE LOG

DIVE No.

Date

Dive Site — Boat/Shore/Inland (circle)

Buddy — Purpose

Boat — Skipper — Port/Launch Site

Dive No./Day — Day in Sequence — Surface Int. : — Time in : — out :

GAS	Mix	Pressure		Cyl. Size
		In	Out	
Bottom				
Travel				
Deco				

DIVE TIME — mins

MAX DEPTH — m/ft

Visibility — m/ft

Stops .... mins @ .... m/ft .... mins @ .... m/ft .... mins @ .... m/ft

Open Circuit ☐   Semi-Closed ☐   Closed Circuit ☐   Comp/Tables ....

Weight .... kg/lbs   **OK:** Y / N   **(Add/Remove** .... **)**

Suit/Undersuit ....   **Gloves** Y / N   **Hood** Y / N   **Hot / Cold / OK**

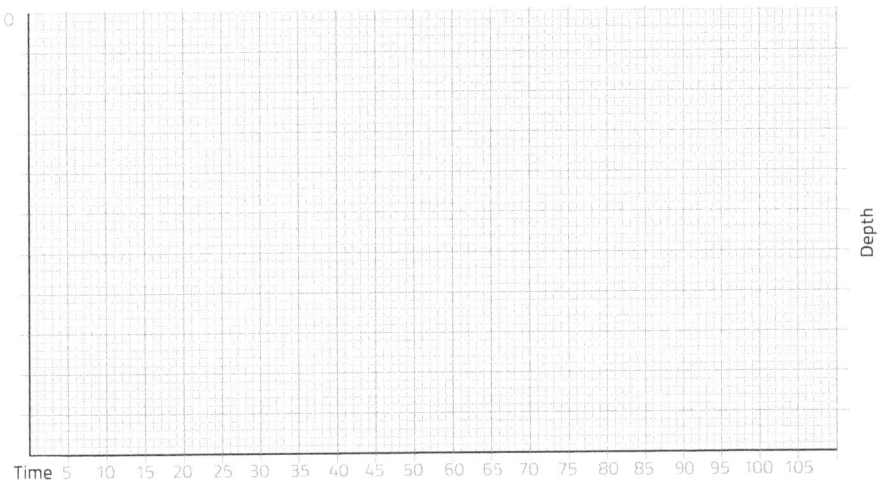

Depth

Time 5 10 15 20 25 30 35 40 45 50 55 60 65 70 75 80 85 90 95 100 105

Summary

Description/Sketch

DIVED UP

Water Speed Slack / Slow / Steady / Fast   Temp @ Depth

Sea State   Wind Speed   Temp@ Surface

Kit/Skills Notes

Accumulated Dive Time   :   Milestone?

Verified by

                                   Signature   No.

DIVE LOG

DIVE No.

Date

Dive Site   Boat/Shore/Inland (circle)

Buddy   Purpose

Boat   **Skipper**   **Port/Launch Site**

| Dive No./Day | Day in Sequence | Surface Int. | : | Time in | : | out | : |

GAS	Mix	Pressure		Cyl. Size
		In	Out	
Bottom				
Travel				
Deco				

DIVE TIME
mins

MAX DEPTH
m/ft

Visibility
m/ft

Stops .... mins @ .... m/ft   .... mins @ .... m/ft   .... mins @ .... m/ft

Open Circuit ☐ **Semi-Closed** ☐ **Closed Circuit** ☐   **Comp/Tables** ....

Weight .... kg/lbs **OK:** Y / N   **(Add/Remove** .... **)**

Suit/Undersuit .... **Gloves** Y / N   **Hood** Y / N   **Hot / Cold / OK**

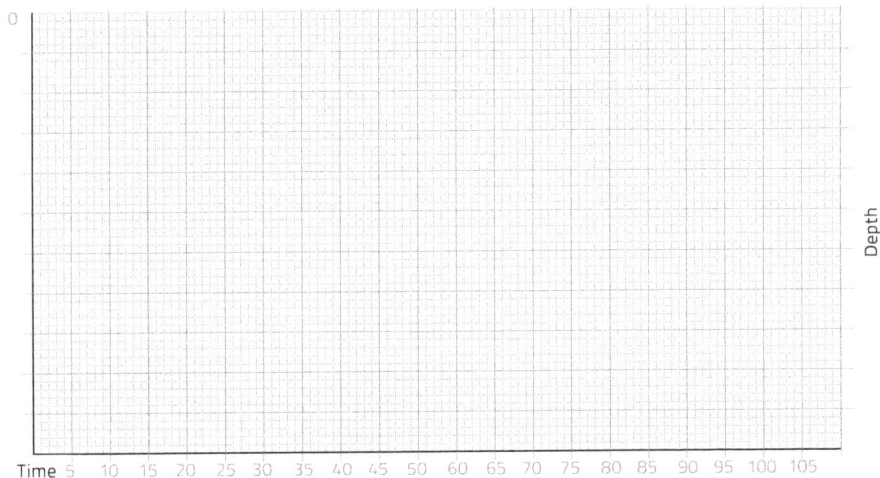

Depth

Time 5   10   15   20   25   30   35   40   45   50   55   60   65   70   75   80   85   90   95   100   105

Summary

Description/Sketch

DIVED UP

Water Speed Slack / Slow / Steady / Fast   Temp @ Depth
Sea State   Wind Speed   Temp@ Surface

Kit/Skills Notes

Accumulated Dive Time   :   Milestone?

Verified by

                              Signature   No.

DIVE LOG

DIVE No.

Date

Dive Site   Boat/Shore/Inland (circle)

Buddy   Purpose

Boat   Skipper   Port/Launch Site

Dive No./Day		Day in Sequence		Surface Int.	:	Time in	:	out	:

GAS	Mix	Pressure		Cyl. Size
		In	Out	
Bottom				
Travel				
Deco				

DIVE TIME   **MAX DEPTH**

mins   m/ft

Visibility

m/ft

Stops .... mins @ .... m/ft   .... mins @ .... m/ft   .... mins @ .... m/ft

Open Circuit   **Semi-Closed**   **Closed Circuit**   **Comp/Tables** ....

Weight ....kg/lbs   **OK:** Y / N   **(Add/Remove** ....**)**

Suit/Undersuit ....**Gloves** Y / N   **Hood** Y / N   **Hot / Cold / OK**

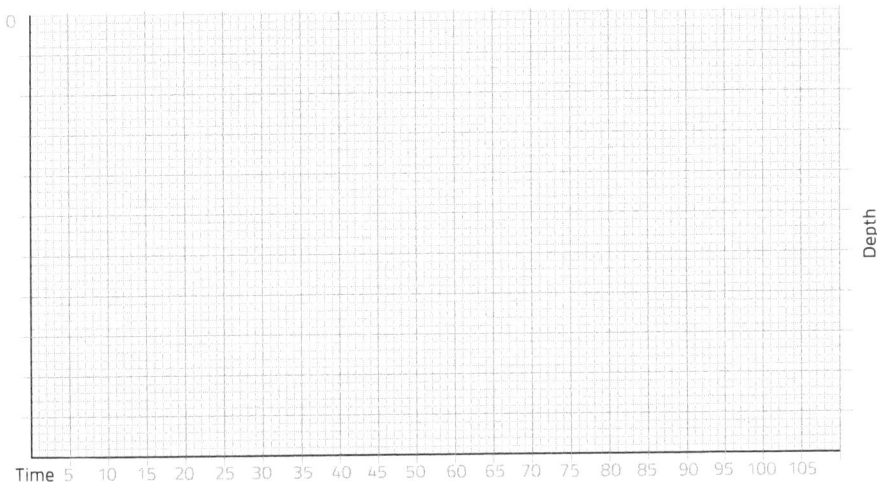

0

Depth

Time 5   10   15   20   25   30   35   40   45   50   60   65   70   75   80   85   90   95   100 105

Summary

Description/Sketch

DIVED UP

Water Speed Slack / Slow / Steady / Fast		Temp @ Depth	
Sea State	Wind Speed	Temp@ Surface	

Kit/Skills Notes

Accumulated Dive Time	:	Milestone?

Verified by

Signature   No.

| DIVE No. | DIVE LOG | Date |

Dive Site — Boat/Shore/Inland (circle)

Buddy — Purpose

Boat — Skipper — Port/Launch Site

Dive No./Day | Day in Sequence | Surface Int. : | Time in : | out :

GAS	Mix	Pressure		Cyl. Size
		In	Out	
Bottom				
Travel				
Deco				

DIVE TIME — mins

MAX DEPTH — m/ft

Visibility — m/ft

Stops .... mins @ .... m/ft .... mins @ .... m/ft .... mins @ .... m/ft

Open Circuit ☐ Semi-Closed ☐ Closed Circuit ☐ Comp/Tables ....

Weight ....kg/lbs **OK:** Y / N (Add/Remove ....)

Suit/Undersuit .... **Gloves** Y / N **Hood** Y / N **Hot / Cold / OK**

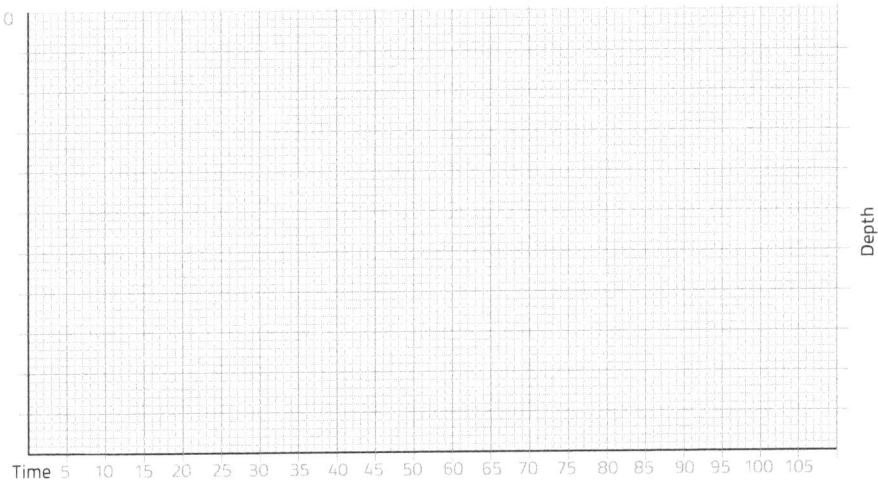

0

Depth

Time 5 10 15 20 25 30 35 40 45 50 60 65 70 75 80 85 90 95 100 105

Summary

Description/Sketch

DIVED UP

Water Speed   Slack / Slow / Steady / Fast   Temp @ Depth

Sea State   Wind Speed   Temp@ Surface

Kit/Skills Notes

Accumulated Dive Time   :   Milestone?

Verified by

Signature   No.

DIVE No.	**DIVE LOG**	Date

Dive Site	Boat/Shore/Inland (circle)

Buddy	Purpose

Boat	Skipper	Port/Launch Site

Dive No./Day		Day in Sequence		Surface Int. :	Time in :	out :

GAS	Mix	Pressure		Cyl. Size
		In	Out	
Bottom				
Travel				
Deco				

DIVE TIME _____ mins

MAX DEPTH _____ m/ft

Visibility _____ m/ft

Stops .... mins @ .... m/ft .... mins @ .... m/ft .... mins @ .... m/ft

Open Circuit ☐   Semi-Closed ☐   Closed Circuit ☐   Comp/Tables ....

Weight ....kg/lbs   OK: Y / N   (Add/Remove.............)

Suit/Undersuit ....Gloves Y / N   Hood Y / N   Hot / Cold / OK

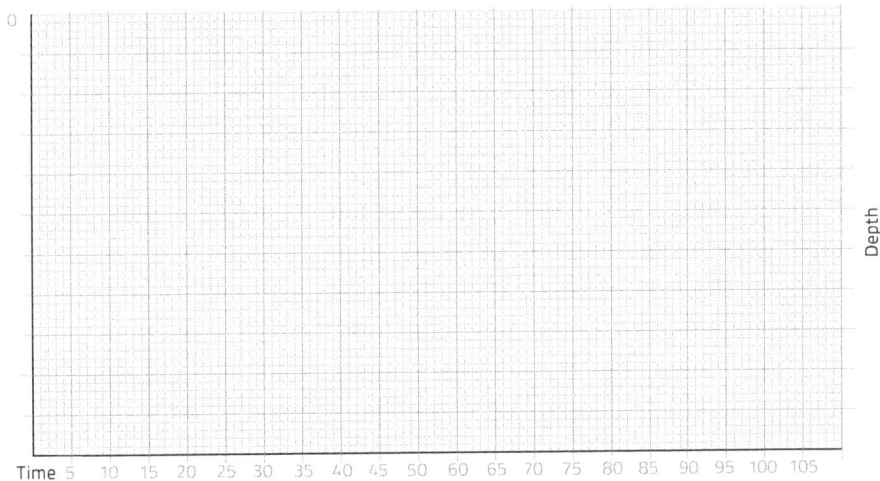

0

Depth

Time 5 10 15 20 25 30 35 40 45 50 55 60 65 70 75 80 85 90 95 100 105

Summary

Description/Sketch

DIVED UP

Water Speed Slack / Slow / Steady / Fast   Temp @ Depth

Sea State   Wind Speed   Temp@ Surface

Kit/Skills Notes

Accumulated Dive Time   :   Milestone?

Verified by

                                    Signature   No.

DIVE No.	DIVE LOG	Date

Dive Site — Boat/Shore/Inland (circle)

Buddy — Purpose

Boat — Skipper — Port/Launch Site

Dive No./Day	Day in Sequence	Surface Int. :	Time in :	out :

GAS	Mix	Pressure		Cyl. Size
		In	Out	
Bottom				
Travel				
Deco				

DIVE TIME	MAX DEPTH
mins	m/ft

Visibility — m/ft

Stops .... mins @ .... m/ft .... mins @ .... m/ft .... mins @ .... m/ft

Open Circuit ☐ Semi-Closed ☐ Closed Circuit ☐ Comp/Tables ....

Weight .... kg/lbs **OK:** Y / N (Add/Remove ....)

Suit/Undersuit .... **Gloves** Y / N **Hood** Y / N **Hot / Cold / OK**

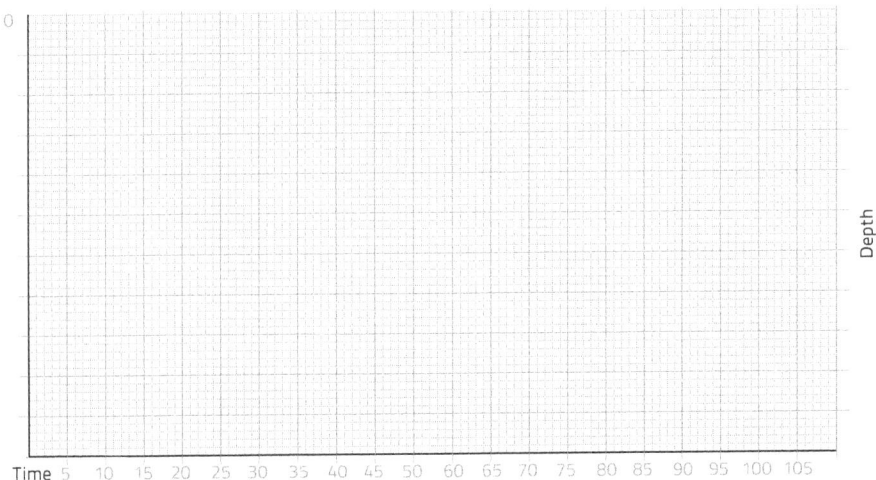

0

Depth

Time 5 10 15 20 25 30 35 40 45 50 60 65 70 75 80 85 90 95 100 105

Summary

Description/Sketch

_____
_____
_____
_____
_____
_____
_____
_____
_____
_____
_____
_____
_____
_____

DIVED UP

Water Speed	Slack / Slow / Steady / Fast	Temp @ Depth
Sea State	Wind Speed	Temp@ Surface

Kit/Skills Notes

Accumulated Dive Time	:	Milestone?

Verified by

Signature   No.

| DIVE No. | **DIVE LOG** | Date |

| **Dive Site** | Boat/Shore/Inland (circle) |

| Buddy | Purpose |

| Boat | Skipper | Port/Launch Site |

| Dive No./Day | Day in Sequence | Surface Int. : | Time in : | out : |

GAS	Mix	Pressure		Cyl. Size
		In	Out	
Bottom				
Travel				
Deco				

DIVE TIME

mins

MAX DEPTH

m/ft

Visibility

m/ft

Stops .... mins @ .... m/ft .... mins @ .... m/ft .... mins @ .... m/ft

Open Circuit ☐ Semi-Closed ☐ Closed Circuit ☐ Comp/Tables ....

Weight .... kg/lbs **OK:** Y / N **(Add/Remove** .... **)**

Suit/Undersuit .... **Gloves** Y / N **Hood** Y / N **Hot / Cold / OK**

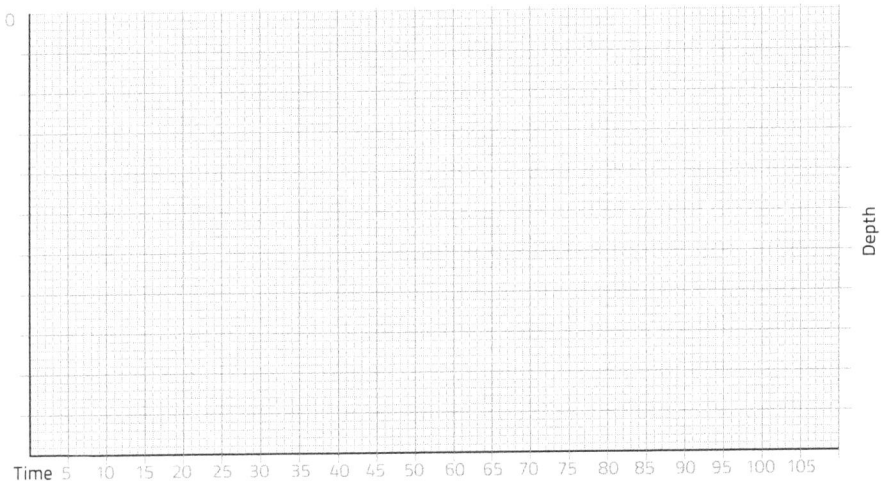

0

Depth

Time 5 10 15 20 25 30 35 40 45 50 60 65 70 75 80 85 90 95 100 105

Summary

Description/Sketch

DIVED UP

Water Speed Slack / Slow / Steady / Fast

Temp @ Depth

Sea State

Wind Speed

Temp@ Surface

Kit/Skills Notes

Accumulated Dive Time :

Milestone?

Verified by

Signature

No.

DIVE No.	**DIVE LOG**	Date

Dive Site | Boat/Shore/Inland (circle)

Buddy | Purpose

Boat | Skipper | Port/Launch Site

| Dive No./Day | | Day in Sequence | | Surface Int. | : | Time in | : | out | : |

GAS	Mix	Pressure		Cyl. Size	**DIVE TIME**	**MAX DEPTH**
		In	Out			
Bottom						
Travel					mins	m/ft
Deco					**Visibility**	
						m/ft

Stops .... mins @ .... m/ft .... mins @ .... m/ft .... mins @ .... m/ft

Open Circuit ☐ Semi-Closed ☐ Closed Circuit ☐ Comp/Tables ....

Weight .... kg/lbs **OK:** Y / N (Add/Remove ....)

Suit/Undersuit .... Gloves Y / N Hood Y / N Hot / Cold / OK

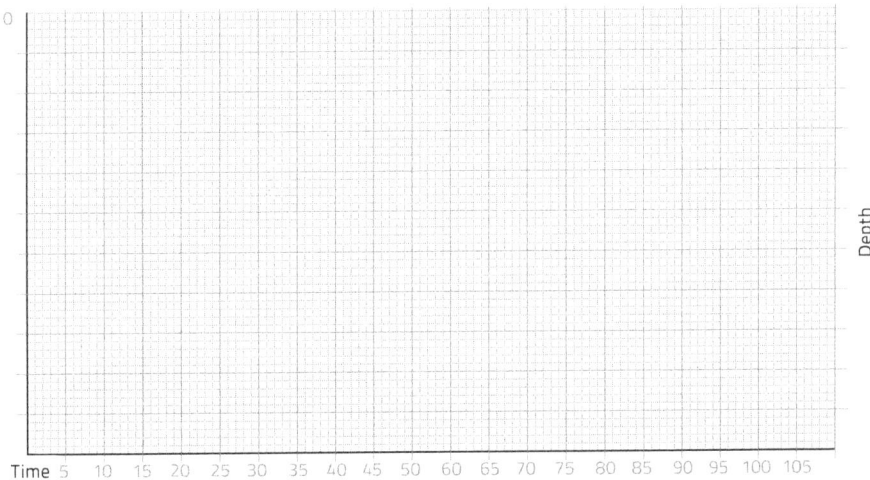

0

Depth

Time 5 10 15 20 25 30 35 40 45 50 55 60 65 70 75 80 85 90 95 100 105

Summary

Description/Sketch

DIVED UP

Water Speed Slack / Slow / Steady / Fast   Temp @ Depth

Sea State   Wind Speed   Temp@ Surface

Kit/Skills Notes

Accumulated Dive Time   :   Milestone?

Verified by

Signature   No.

DIVE No.	**DIVE LOG**	Date

Dive Site Boat/Shore/Inland (circle)

Buddy Purpose

Boat Skipper Port/Launch Site

Dive No./Day	Day in Sequence	Surface Int :	Time in :	out :

GAS	Mix	Pressure		Cyl. Size
		In	Out	
Bottom				
Travel				
Deco				

DIVE TIME	**MAX DEPTH**
mins	m/ft

Visibility m/ft

Stops .... mins @ .... m/ft .... mins @ .... m/ft .... mins @ .... m/ft

Open Circuit ☐ Semi-Closed ☐ Closed Circuit ☐ Comp/Tables ....

Weight ....kg/lbs **OK:** Y / N **(Add/Remove** .... **)**

Suit/Undersuit ....**Gloves** Y / N **Hood** Y / N **Hot / Cold / OK**

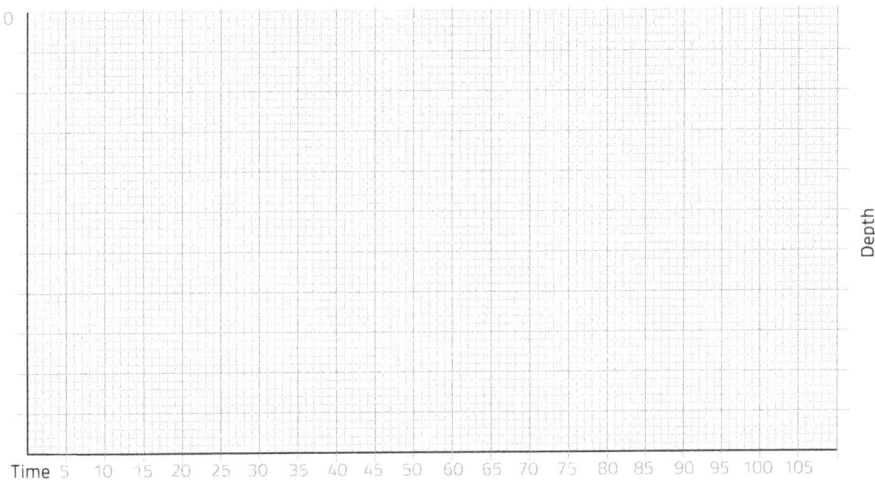

0

Depth

Time 5 10 15 20 25 30 35 40 45 50 55 60 65 70 75 80 85 90 95 100 105

Summary

Description/Sketch

DIVED UP

Water Speed Slack / Slow / Steady / Fast	Temp @ Depth
Sea State Wind Speed	Temp@ Surface

Kit/Skills Notes

Accumulated Dive Time :	Milestone?

Verified by

Signature   No.

DIVE No.	DIVE LOG	Date

Dive Site | Boat/Shore/Inland (circle)

Buddy | Purpose

Boat | Skipper | Port/Launch Site

Dive No./Day	Day in Sequence	Surface Int. :	Time in :	out :

GAS	Mix	Pressure		Cyl. Size
		In	Out	
Bottom				
Travel				
Deco				

DIVE TIME

mins

MAX DEPTH

m/ft

Visibility

m/ft

Stops .... mins @ .... m/ft .... mins @ .... m/ft .... mins @ .... m/ft

Open Circuit	Semi-Closed	Closed Circuit	Comp/Tables ....

Weight .... kg/lbs **OK:** Y / N **(Add/Remove** .... **)**

Suit/Undersuit .... **Gloves** Y / N **Hood** Y / N **Hot / Cold / OK**

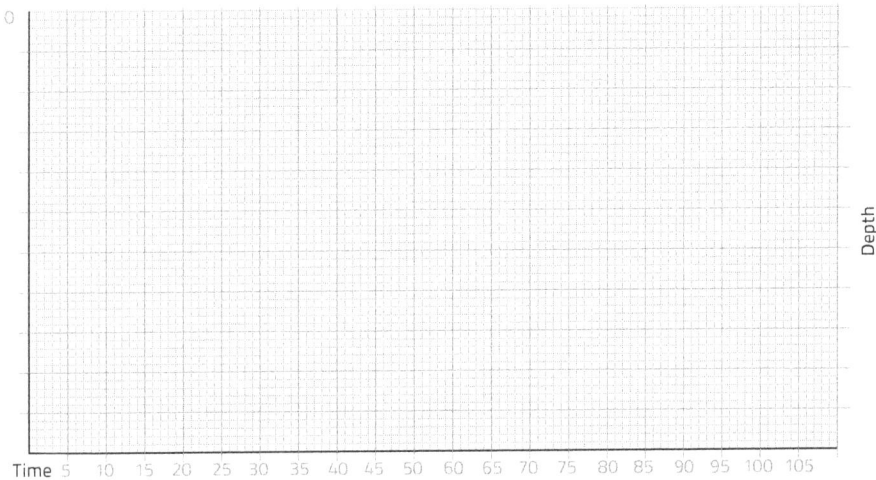

0

Depth

Time 5   10   15   20   25   30   35   40   45   50   60   65   70   75   80   85   90   95   100 105

Summary

Description/Sketch

DIVED UP

Water Speed Slack / Slow / Steady / Fast   Temp @ Depth
Sea State   Wind Speed   Temp@ Surface

Kit/Skills Notes

Accumulated Dive Time   :   Milestone?

Verified by

Signature   No.

DIVE No.	**DIVE LOG**	Date

Dive Site   Boat/Shore/Inland (circle)

Buddy   Purpose

Boat   Skipper   Port/Launch Site

| Dive No./Day | | Day in Sequence | | Surface Int. | : | Time in | : | out | : |

GAS	Mix	Pressure		Cyl. Size
		In	Out	
Bottom				
Travel				
Deco				

DIVE TIME   **MAX DEPTH**

mins   m/ft

Visibility
m/ft

Stops .... mins @ .... m/ft   .... mins @ .... m/ft   .... mins @ .... m/ft

Open Circuit   **Semi-Closed**   **Closed Circuit**   **Comp/Tables** ....
Weight ....kg/lbs   **OK:** Y / N   **(Add/Remove** ....**)**
Suit/Undersuit ....**Gloves** Y / N   **Hood** Y / N   **Hot / Cold / OK**

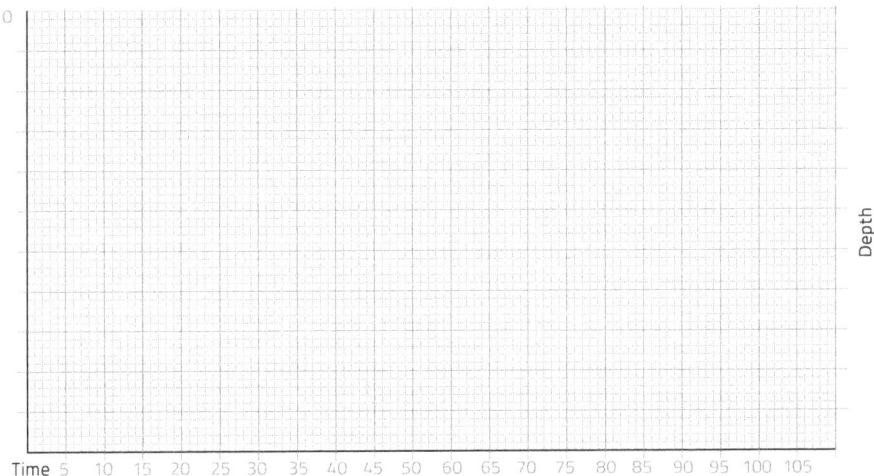

0

Depth

Time 5   10   15   20   25   30   35   40   45   50   55   60   65   70   75   80   85   90   95   100   105

Summary

Description/Sketch

DIVED UP

Kit/Skills Notes

Accumulated Dive Time   :   Milestone?

Verified by

Signature   No.

DIVE LOG

DIVE No.

Date

Dive Site   Boat/Shore/Inland (circle)

Buddy   Purpose

Boat   Skipper   Port/Launch Site

| Dive No./Day | | Day in Sequence | | Surface Int. | : | Time in | : | out | : |

GAS	Mix	Pressure		Cyl. Size
		In	Out	
Bottom				
Travel				
Deco				

DIVE TIME

mins

MAX DEPTH

m/ft

Visibility

m/ft

Stops .... mins @ .... m/ft .... mins @ .... m/ft .... mins @ .... m/ft

Open Circuit ☐ **Semi-Closed** ☐ **Closed Circuit** ☐ **Comp/Tables** ....

Weight .... kg/lbs **OK:** Y / N **(Add/Remove** .... **)**

Suit/Undersuit .... **Gloves** Y / N **Hood** Y / N **Hot / Cold / OK**

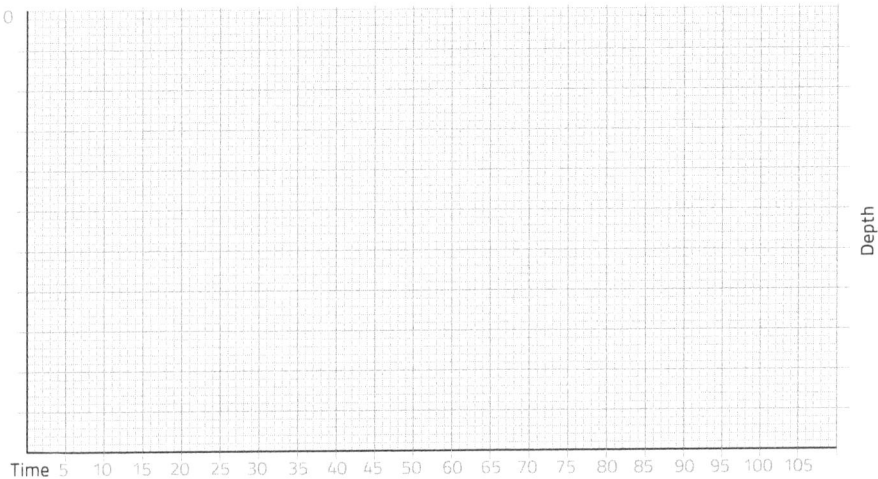

0

Depth

Time 5 10 15 20 25 30 35 40 45 50 55 60 65 70 75 80 85 90 95 100 105

Summary

Description/Sketch

DIVED UP

Water Speed Slack / Slow / Steady / Fast	Temp @ Depth
Sea State Wind Speed	Temp@ Surface

Kit/Skills Notes

Accumulated Dive Time :	Milestone?

Verified by

Signature   No.

NOTES

Winning Images with ANY Underwater Camera
The Essential Guide to Creating Engaging Photos
by Paul Colley, with a Foreword by Alex Mustard

'For all underwater photographers who want to get ahead of the game': *UWP Magazine*

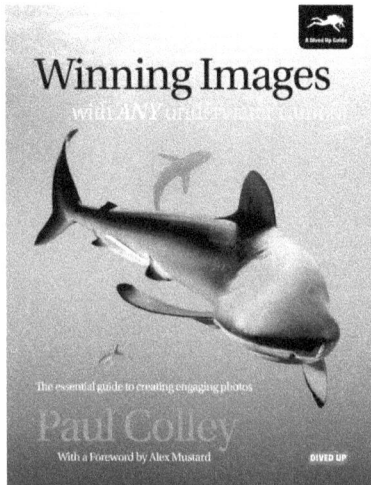

'Excellently written, highly informative and well-executed… the essential guide on this subject': *Diver magazine*

'Will arm and inspire you to transform your underwater photographs, whatever camera you use': Alex Mustard

- Learn how to take photos like the pros
- Secrets of great composition revealed
- One book, any camera

2014 | Paperback and Ebook | ISBN 978-1-909455-04-7

For more details and to order go to **DivedUp.com**

.